The River of God

The River of God

Dutch Sheets

Renew

**A Division of Gospel Light
Ventura, California, U.S.A.**

Published by Regal Books
From Gospel Light
Ventura, California, U.S.A.
Printed in the U.S.A.

Regal Books is a ministry of Gospel Light, an evangelical Christian publisher dedicated to serving the local church. We believe God's vision for Gospel Light is to provide church leaders with biblical, user-friendly materials that will help them evangelize, disciple and minister to children, youth and families.

It is our prayer that this Regal book will help you discover biblical truth for your own life and help you meet the needs of others. May God richly bless you.

For a free catalog of resources from Regal Books/Gospel Light please call your Christian supplier or contact us at 1-800-4-GOSPEL, or at www.gospellight.com.

Cover Design by Barbara LeVan Fisher
Interior Design by Britt Rocchio
Edited by David Webb

Library of Congress Cataloging-in-Publication Data
Sheets, Dutch.
    The river of God / Dutch Sheets.
            p.   cm.
    Includes bibliographical references.
    ISBN 0-8307-2075-8 (Trade paperback)
    1. Christian life.   I. Title.
    BV4501.2.S4357   1998   98-21603
    243—dc21   CIP

6 7 8 9 10 11 12 13 14 15 16 17 18 19 20 21 22 23 / 08 07 06 05 04 03

Rights for publishing this book in other languages are contracted by Gospel Light Worldwide, the international nonprofit ministry of Gospel Light. Gospel Light Worldwide also provides publishing and technical assistance to international publishers dedicated to producing Sunday School and Vacation Bible School curricula and books in the languages of the world. For additional information, visit www.gospellightworldwide.org; write to Gospel Light Worldwide, P.O. Box 3875, Ventura, CA 93006; or send an e-mail to info@gospellightworldwide.org.

—

The Sheets household—
Dutch, Ceci, Sarah and Hannah—
lovingly dedicate this book to the memory of the Cross,
where we were plunged beneath the flood
and lost our guilty stains.

"Jesus, my heart is forever Yours!" — Ceci

"Jesus, You're the best!" — Sarah

"Jesus, I love You!" — Hannah

"Dittos!" — Dutch

—

Contents

Foreword

I have studied the Reformation, revivals, renewal movements and other moves of God for almost thirty years. I have visited such movements and spent a good deal of time with some of the men and women who have been used to start them. Some characteristics seem to be common to all these movements, but in many ways they are all unique. The God who made every snowflake different obviously loves diversity.

One of the great revivals now taking place was actually planned by its leaders. That may be shocking to revival idealists— who tend to think that if men had anything to do with revival, it could not be of God—but that is not so. What the leaders of this revival did was out of wisdom. They discerned what the Lord was going to do and planned accordingly. They were ready for the move of God, and it probably has been more effective as a result.

Other friends of mine were used to start a worldwide renewal movement that started very differently. When this renewal broke out, the leaders were as surprised as anyone. The grace of God was with them, however, and they have been able to administrate the movement exceptionally well. Both of these movements are very different, but both have been greatly used by God.

Now it seems that almost everyone has a vision for some sort of revival, reformation or renewal. This is encouraging. Vision is a powerful force. Almost all human advancement is the result of someone

having a vision. Most people have a vision of what they want to do
or be. For some this is little more than a daydream; for others it has
evolved into a detailed plan. Even so, very few fulfill their vision.

Vision alone has never accomplished anything. Between the
place of having a vision and seeing the vision fulfilled, there will
usually be a lot of hard work that few visionaries have been willing to do. That is why, regardless of how good a person's vision
sounds, I will not be too encouraged about it until I see them
demonstrating a heart for work. Having the vision is the fun part.
Walking it out is usually much more difficult. This is why James
wrote, "For just as the body without the spirit is dead, so also
faith without works is dead" (Jas. 2:26).

Spiritual vision is more than just having great or noble ideas.
True spiritual vision can only come from being able to see with
God's eyes. Even so, that is still the fun part. Seeing what the Lord
wants to do is essential, but working with Him to accomplish it
is just as important. This is why I am encouraged by this book.
The author, Dutch Sheets, is not just a visionary, but one who is
also committed to doing the work. His books contain more than
vision; they are also practical.

Implying that men must do work in revival is an offense to
some idealists, but God has chosen to work through men. That is
why moves of the Holy Spirit are called "outpourings" instead of
"downpourings." True moves of the Holy Spirit will come
through His people. This is not to imply that revivals or moves of
God are the result of human strength or striving. Only the Spirit
can beget that which is spirit. However, we do work *with* God.
As the Lord said in Matthew 11:28-30:

Come to Me, all who are weary and heavy-laden, and I will
give you rest. Take My yoke upon you, and learn from Me,
for I am gentle and humble in heart; and you shall find rest
for your souls. For My yoke is easy, and My load is light.

A yoke implies work, but when we are yoked with Him, it will
be His strength doing the pulling. The work we do with Him will

..... praise for THE RIVER OF GOD ......

Dutch Sheets has written a wonderful new book
filled with outstanding illustrations and insights into
Scripture. I highly recommend *The River of God.*

Dr. Ché Ahn

SENIOR PASTOR, HARVEST ROCK CHURCH
PASADENA, CALIFORNIA

Dutch Sheets is a prophet with a strong teaching gift.
This has come forth powerfully in his book, *Intercessory
Prayer*, and in the course by that name he teaches at
Beacon College. Now that same anointing flows again in
The River of God. Robust exegesis and strong word study
are made easy, even enjoyable, by Dutch's down-home
manner and unique humor. We are in the season of
harvest. The full river of God's anointing is here.
This book will help all of us "let the river flow."
It is a must read. I heartily recommend it.

Ronald E. Cottle

PRESIDENT, BEACON COLLEGE, CHRISTIAN LIFE SCHOOL
OF THEOLOGY, COLUMBUS, GEORGIA

Revival—a word that has stirred both curiosity
and controversy, as well as fresh excitement and
anticipation in God's people in this hour. With clarity,
depth and passion, Dutch once again unfolds balanced
scriptural truths that will bring understanding to this vital
move of God's Spirit. If you've been thirsting
after more of God, this book is for you!

Jane Hansen

AUTHOR OF *FASHIONED FOR INTIMACY*
PRESIDENT/CEO, AGLOW INTERNATIONAL
EDMONDS, WASHINGTON

Insightful! Inspirational! Informative! This new book by
Dutch Sheets could very well be the vehicle that moves the
Church from experiencing a few mercy drops of spiritual
renewal to a mighty deluge of spiritual awakening! Make use
of this exegetically excellent, yet very readable work to stir
your own heart and to teach others.

Jim Hodges
PRESIDENT, FEDERATION OF MINISTERS AND CHURCHES, INC.
DUNCANVILLE, TEXAS

This book is a vehicle that will allow the Holy Spirit to
dig deeply into the trenches of your heart in order for the
power of God to flow through you. It is written in the
fresh, classic Sheets style—down to earth, but in touch
with God. *The River of God* will cause you to thirst after
righteousness and will change you forever.

Cindy Jacobs
AUTHOR OF *THE VOICE OF GOD* AND *WOMEN OF DESTINY*
COFOUNDER, GENERALS OF INTERCESSION
COLORADO SPRINGS, COLORADO

Dutch Sheets has a fresh, in-depth revelation that is
well worth reading—even for a second and third time.
The River of God flows from the heart of God and
penetrates into the innermost depths of the reader. This
book is for the "Marthas" who want to be "Marys," who
have found themselves so busy working for God that
they are unable to have fun and enjoy the presence of
their Creator. It is not just another book about revival;
it is a book for spiritual resuscitation.

Dennis Lindsay
CHAIRMAN OF THE BOARD, PRESIDENT AND CEO
CHRIST FOR THE NATIONS, DALLAS, TEXAS

This book is strong medicine! It is not for the
nonchalant, the status quo or the business-as-usual
individual who is only in up to his ankles.
The River of God is a book for the strong swimmers
who are determined to make it safely to the other
side, and will also rescue a host to go with them.
Stepping into the flow of God's river affords the
opportunity for being a vital force in this end-time
revival. But at what cost? In this book, Sheets has
carefully detailed the price from the Bible. Rivers
create new channels. Are you willing and ready for
changes? If you are ready to go the distance,
read *The River of God* and enjoy the swim.

Freda Lindsay

COFOUNDER OF CHRIST FOR THE NATIONS
DALLAS, TEXAS

It is evident that Pastor Dutch Sheets has received
a clear revelation that "The River" is God Himself.
God flowed His life and love into His Son, Jesus,
through whom flows the water of Life. Then through
God's heavenly dynamo—the Holy Spirit—He flows
into and out of Spirit-filled believers' rivers of living
water. Sheets teaches us how to find that river,
which is loaded with fish—the souls of men who
will be swept into the kingdom of God through
the coming revival. All who read these pages will
be changed by this timely revelation of God.

Dr. Fuchsia T. Pickett

BLOUNTVILLE, TENNESSEE

Dutch Sheets once again captures the heart of God
in portraying spiritual life. He draws us to the Author
of the River and not just the River itself. The process
of life in this book causes readers to be propelled
toward their destiny and purpose in God.
The waters of revival are stirring. Jump in by reading
The River of God, be made whole and walk out
your mission of harvest on this earth.

Chuck D. Pierce

DIRECTOR, WORLD PRAYER CENTER
COLORADO SPRINGS, COLORADO

⟨~~~~⟩

There are two reasons I endorse this book:
(1) I know the author. Dutch Sheets is my friend,
brother and son. I watched as he became a part
of the river and the river a part of him.
(2) Dutch wields a sharp sword! But with it he
points the way to the many rainbows of
God's roaring river of revival.

Pastor Dean Sheets (Pappy)

FATHER OF DUTCH SHEETS
THE LIVING WORD, MIDDLETOWN, OHIO

⟨~~~~⟩

Challenging. Poignant. Funny. Heartrending.
Dutch Sheets makes you want to rush to the river of
God with a thirsty heart ready for whatever repentance
is required to experience a personal revival. You will be
stretched and enriched in your Christian walk as you
read this much-needed book.

Quin Sherrer

AUTHOR OF *HOW TO PRAY FOR YOUR CHILDREN* AND *A WOMAN'S
GUIDE TO SPIRITUAL WARFARE*, COLORADO SPRINGS, COLORADO

The River of God is deep, biblical and well researched,
yet written with humor and life flowing out of it.
You will find it entertaining as well as edifying.
As one who came into a fresh flow of God during
the charismatic movement, reading the book has
stirred up a deep longing in my heart to reach a more
intimate relationship with God and to be carried
along in His river. Thank you, Dutch!

Willard Thiessen

COHOST, CANADIAN TV PROGRAM "IT'S A NEW DAY"
WINNIPEG, MANITOBA, CANADA

~

Have you ever wondered why most revivals you have
heard of don't last very long? Dutch Sheets has given
us some amazing biblical and practical answers to that
perplexing question. *The River of God* is one of the
most important books about revival that I have yet seen.

C. Peter Wagner

FULLER THEOLOGICAL SEMINARY
COLORADO SPRINGS, COLORADO

~

be the most fulfilling, refreshing thing we can do. However, any way you look at it, there is work to be done. That is why we are called "laborers" in the harvest. That is why in the places where you find the greatest revivals, you will always find the hardest workers. As long as the workers are staying yoked with the Lord, their labors will always result in the refreshing of their souls, and the revival will stay on track.

In ancient Israel, the Ark of the Covenant represented the glory and presence of the Lord. One of King David's greatest achievements was to bring the Ark to Jerusalem. There he placed it in an open tent so that all the people could behold it. He called together and supported thousands of singers so that there would be continuous worship before the Lord. This worship lasted for 33 years, one for each year that Jesus would walk the earth, so that the glory of God could be openly beheld by all men.

David's Tabernacle was one of the most simple, yet most glorious, of the dwelling places of God in the Scriptures. It is also the only one that the Lord promised to rebuild (see Amos 9:11).

King David did bring the Ark to Jerusalem, but the story did not begin as a happy one. He thought he could bring the Ark to Jerusalem on a new oxcart. I can identify with that. I love innovation, and I love to try things that have not been done before. Some of our innovations the Lord has blessed, and a couple He has visited with His manifest presence. Even so, the glory of the Lord will not come because we invent some snappy new way to do things.

In Scripture, oxen often represent natural strength. When David sought to bring home the Ark with a new oxcart, it was an affront to the holiness of God. When the cart began to totter, Uzzah, whose name means "strength," reached out to steady the Ark and was struck dead for his presumption. We will never be able to steady the glory of God with our own strength.

David was stunned by God's outburst against Uzzah, and the whole procession was stopped. They moved the Ark into the house of Obed-edom, which we can assume they did very carefully. But David did not give up. He went back and studied how the Lord had decreed for the Ark of His presence to be moved. The king returned in greater humility, but with no less resolution. With him he brought the Levites, whom God had designated to carry His Ark. Once again, they began the journey up to Jerusalem.

> Now it was told King David, saying "The Lord has blessed the house of Obed-edom and all that belongs to him, on account of the ark of God." And David went and brought up the ark of God from the house of Obed-edom into the city of David with gladness.
>
> And so it was, that when the bearers of the ark of the Lord had gone six paces, he sacrificed an ox and a fatling.
>
> And David was dancing before the Lord with all his might, and David was wearing a linen ephod. So David and all the house of Israel were bringing up the ark of the Lord with shouting and the sound of the trumpet.
>
> Then it happened as the ark of the Lord came into the city of David that Michal the daughter of Saul looked out of the window and saw King David leaping and dancing before the Lord; and she despised him in her heart.
>
> So they brought in the ark of the Lord and set it in its place inside the tent which David had pitched for it; and David offered burnt offerings and peace offerings before the Lord. And when David had finished offering the burnt offering and the peace offering, he blessed the people in the name of the Lord of hosts (2 Sam. 6:12-18).

This is truly an amazing and wonderful story. We can imagine the pageantry, the music and, of course, seeing King David dancing with all his might before the Lord. However, one of the most important aspects of this story is often overlooked. Verse 13 says:

> And so it was, that when the bearers of the ark of the Lord had gone six paces, he sacrificed an ox and a fatling.

The procession, led by King David, stopped *every six paces* to sacrifice an ox and a fatling! I asked a friend who lives near the ancient sight of Obed-edom's house how far it was from there to Mount Zion where the Ark was taken. He estimates that it was between 12 and 15 kilometers. It would take a man about 30,000 paces to cover that distance. That means they stopped more than 3,500 times to make sacrifices in order to carry the Ark to Mount Zion!

Six is the number of man (man was created on the sixth day) and the ox represents natural strength. Fatlings were considered the finest meat that could be served. For David to bring the Ark home required a continual sacrifice of that which represented his own strength and the very best meat that could be served.

When we gain a new insight from Scripture, or discover a new way of doing things that God seems to bless, it is easy to think we can make a new oxcart out of it, attach it to the ox (our own natural strength) and we will be the ones to bring the glory in. This is a profound and potentially costly delusion. From Obed-edom's house to Mount Zion, the procession left in its wake a trail of blood and guts as far as the eye could see. It was not a pretty picture. No wonder David was dancing with all of his might when they finally made it through the gates!

The best new oxcart will never be good enough to carry the glory of God. The best teachings, meetings and conferences will not get us home. We must give ourselves to the continual sacrifice of our own strength, offering only the very finest meat. However, regardless of the price, we cannot settle for anything less than seeing the glory of the Lord openly revealed in the midst of His people. Above all things, we must have the manifest presence of the Lord. As Moses said to God in Exodus 33:13-16:

"Now therefore, I pray Thee, if I have found favor in Thy sight, let me know Thy ways, that I may know Thee, so that I may find favor in Thy sight. Consider too, that this nation is Thy people."

And He said, "My presence shall go with you, and I will give you rest."

Then he said to Him, "If Thy presence does not go with us, do not lead us up from here. For how then can it be known that I have found favor in Thy sight, I and Thy people? Is it not by Thy going with us, so that we, I and Thy people, may be distinguished from all the other people who are upon the face of the earth?"

Christianity is more than just a better way to live, or a more accurate teaching about God. True Christianity means a relationship with God; it is to become the temple of the Holy Spirit. He does abide in all who have been born again by His Spirit, but is He manifested through us? This is what we seek, to have the sweet aroma of the knowledge of God manifested through us in every place (see 2 Cor. 2:14).

King David loved the Lord's presence so much, he said he would never be able to rest until the Lord had a place to rest. He would make mistakes in trying to bring the Ark home, but there was no price too great for him to pay, no drudgery too difficult for him to have the Lord's presence with him. How many others would have lasted through ten sacrifices? Is it possible there were even many who would have endured a thousand? That was only the beginning for David. Do we really want the Ark that badly? Such a course is intended to separate the idealists and visionaries from those who really are after God's own heart.

Even for David, a pioneering, adventurous type, the plodding trek up the mountain must have been one of the greatest tests of patience he ever endured. The way the Lord has prescribed for the Ark of His presence to be carried is probably designed for tempering just such a nature. Only those who are of such a pioneering nature would even attempt to bring the Ark to their home, but until that nature is tempered so that it moves in perfect step with the Lord, it can cause us to hurt people, as the tragic loss of Uzzah testified. Boldness is one of the great manifestations of a faith that pleases God, but without tempering it can be deadly. It is the blending of boldness with obedience that will be most likely to see the glory of God.

—Rick Joyner

CHAPTER ONE

Experiencing the River

Rivers can be peaceful, violent, lots of fun and sometimes deadly. I've had several interesting river experiences. I remember floating down the Zambezi River in Zimbabwe. This was when the country was called Rhodesia and was embroiled in a great internal conflict between the whites and blacks. Due to the constant threat of terrorism, an army patrol boat continually circled us, watching for terrorists. A nice, relaxing cruise!

Then there was my trip down the Passion River in Guatemala, where an army of voracious ants crawled onto me as I lay sleeping on the boat. (Don't ask me how they got in the boat; maybe they were swimming ants.) When they were all in position, the ants began to bite all at once and with incredible precision. Actually, *gnaw* would be more accurate. Fifteen screams, one boat-rearranging conniption fit and several dozen dead ants later, I regained my peace like the man of God I am and went back to sleep. Just like Jesus, sleeping through the storm.

Another time, I went skiing on the Ohio River near Cincinnati. I was in the water, not yet up on my skis, when my friend at the helm decided the barge was getting a mite too close. My buddy hit the throttle, and I grabbed the rope. Leaving my skis behind, I was dragged headfirst across the Ohio River out of harm's way. It was a real drag.

Last, but not least, there was the time my buddies and I tried to drive a Jeep across the Miami River in Ohio—it was a bit deeper than it looked. We thought we might be in a little trouble when the engine died, but the significance of that faded when *the Jeep began to float*. My buddy had these huge tires—about eight feet wide and just as tall—and the law of buoyancy had kicked in. We pushed and pulled, finally getting close enough to the bank for the Jeep to sit on the bottom again. Then we all forced a "Boy, that was cool, wasn't it" laugh and bragged about it for the next week at school. I, for one, was glad to be in the water. It camouflaged my true emotional response.

Surprised by the River of God

On March 9, 1997, God put me in *His* river. Though interesting and sometimes even exciting, my previous river adventures pale in contrast to what happened to me on this particular Sunday. Along with several others, I was praying during our regular morning service for the youth in our church. Powerful ministry took place as many were visibly moved upon by the Holy Spirit. Strong anointing was evident with young people weeping, laughing, repenting and falling under God's power. I, too, wept.

Suddenly, someone laid their hands on me and began to pray. I found myself on the floor with some of the young people, receiving what I can only call a vision from God. I lay there for 45 minutes, sometimes laughing and other times weeping, as God took me on a journey. Not being a person particularly given to this sort of thing, it took me completely by surprise.

After all, I'm rather reserved and somewhat cerebral. I'm a teacher. I study. I do word studies, run references. I think didactically. I figure things out. I have to know why, how. My little cerebral, didactic mind wasn't prepared for what was happening. Maybe this surprise invasion of my cranial disposition didn't blow my mind, but it sure stretched it out of shape.

Does it bother you when God does something you can't quite explain or understand? If asked, I'd be the first to say I don't have God or His ways completely figured out. This doesn't bother me. It's when He demonstrates it that I get a little flustered. I'm just like you. I have my comfort zones. I pray, "Lord, send revival, but do it *my* way. Please check with me on the timing, methods and the particular changes revival will require *before* you begin."

He didn't.

As with the wise men who "followed a star and found a stable,"[1] Mary who rocked a son and raised a Savior, and the disciples

—

I found myself in God's river, frolicking with Jesus. This might offend your concept of our Lord, but He was in a very playful mood.

who longed for a crown and looked at a cross, He continues to surprise us.

What happened while I was on the floor was nothing less than amazing to me.

The Vision

I found myself in God's river—a river about waist-deep and perhaps 30 feet wide—frolicking with Jesus. This might offend your concept of our Lord, but He was in a very playful mood. We swam, we splashed, we laughed. He even dunked me! (I *tried* to dunk Him.) We did all the things people do when they play in the water.

At one point Jesus put His head under the water, then came up shaking His head from side to side, throwing water all over me. Intending to do the same to Him, I put my head under the water but was distracted by what happened. As I put my head under the water and began to shake it, impurities were washed off me and began to float downstream. Each time I was immersed in it, the river was cleansing me! As Naaman the leper dipping in the Jordan River (see 2 Kings 5:1-14), God's river was purifying me of my uncleanness.

Another thing I found quite interesting was I couldn't drown in the water. When my head went under and I accidentally breathed in, the water didn't choke me as water typically does. Instead of going into my lungs, causing me to gag and choke, it flowed throughout my entire body, bringing refreshment and vitality. It was, indeed, the river of *life* (see Rev. 22:1).

We continued to frolic for a while, just having fun. I can't overemphasize how much Jesus was enjoying Himself. Psalm 46:4 became a reality to me: "There is a river whose streams make *glad* the city of God, the holy dwelling places of the Most High" (italics mine). Throughout the vision, no matter what we did, Jesus was having fun. Imagine that—God having fun. Until this time, I don't recall the thought entering my mind. I guess I thought He was too cerebral and didactic.

"Let's Splash Them"

A group of people on the shore were watching us. For reasons unknown to me at the time, they were hesitant to get in the water. They seemed to be afraid of it. I realize now this group represented those who are somewhat cautious, or even fearful, of the manifestations of the Holy Spirit accompanying the worldwide move of God so many are calling "the river." (I will discuss these manifestations and the concerns many have about them in a later chapter.)

As these people stood on the shore watching us, trying to decide whether or not to get in the water, the Lord looked at me and said, "Let's splash them." We began to do so and, without exception, when the water touched those on the bank, they wanted to get in the river. It was infectious. Then they, too, started having fun with us. How's that for a paradox? The water not only quenched thirst, but also created it.

At one point I asked Jesus why the water was only waist-deep. I recalled from Ezekiel's vision of God's river in Ezekiel 47 that the river got progressively deeper, "trickling...ankles...knees...loins...enough water to swim in, a river that could not be forded" (Ezek. 47:2-5).

He replied to me that this level was for the Church—for cleansing, refreshing and renewal. "The deeper water," He said, "is what takes the river to the nations." Instantly, the water rose until it was a deep, swift current that swept us away. Though it was strong and overpowered me, I was not afraid. After this demonstration, we were brought back to the original place and water level.

As people were moving in and out of the water, I saw a lady diseased with cancer. Jesus looked at me, smiling. He said rather matter-of-factly, "Well, go heal her." I walked to her and put my hand on her. As I did, the Lord moved behind me and placed His hand in the middle of my back. When He did, power went from Him, through me and into this lady, healing her. We then went back to playing in the river.

Everything Will Live Where the River Goes

Next, the Lord did something unusual and fun. He pointed in front of Him at the water and said, "Watch this." Suddenly a huge geyser spewed about 30 to 40 feet up out of the river and fell back to the surface. This surprised and amused me, but He simply laughed. As before, Jesus was thoroughly enjoying Himself. Looking at me, He said, "Go ahead, get on it." As I stepped to the spot, the geyser shot up again, carrying me high into the air. It held me there for a couple of seconds, then lowered me back into the water. As you can imagine, I was startled, but at no point in the vision was I afraid. By this time, I was feeling somewhat bold so I said, "Get on it with me."

To my pleasant, cerebral surprise, He said, "Okay," and moved beside me. The geyser shot up again, this time carrying both of us skyward. We were laughing and having a blast. (Pun intended.) While we were at the highest point, Christ looked at me and said, "Let's go." As He said this, we were immediately whisked away through the air. I recall seeing the earth below us as we flew off.

The journey seemed to only last a few seconds, and we landed in a small, primitive village of tiny huts with thatched roofs. It reminded me of places I've seen in Africa and Guatemala. We were standing on the edge of the village with the river behind us. Though we did not travel to this place on the river, it was nevertheless there.

The people from the village came and gathered in front of us. They were staring only at me, however, waiting for me to speak. I expected the Lord to do the talking. He looked at me and said, "They can't see Me, as you can. Go ahead and share the gospel with them." I did as He instructed, and the people immediately fell to their knees weeping, receiving Christ into their hearts.

They said to me through their tears, "We knew someone was coming to tell us about God. We've been waiting." I wept also (both in the vision and, as I later discovered, while lying on the floor). Ezekiel 47:9 was made real to me:

> And it will come about that every living creature which swarms in every place where the river goes, will live. And there will be very many fish, for these waters go there, and the others become fresh; so everything will live where the river goes.

The Lord said to me, "Come on, let's go someplace else." Immediately we flew off into the air again. As we traveled, I asked where we were going. He said, "You'll see." We landed in Chernobyl, Russia, where the nuclear reactor blew up in 1986. I do not know why the Lord picked this place. I had not thought of it in years and had never been particularly drawn toward ministering in Russia.

I found myself facing people suffering from great oppression, diseases and birth defects. They stood before me with hopeless, blank expressions on their faces. Then they began to speak, telling me their problems and pains. "So many are bound by alcohol," a woman said. Instantly, there stood before me a man who I knew was an alcoholic.

I said, "That's no problem for the Lord," and put my hand on his head and prayed. Immediately, he was delivered from alcoholism. He, as myself, had been cleansed by the river. He wasn't in it, literally, as I had been; but I knew the power released through me came from the river.

A lady with a small child next to her then spoke to me. "There is so much disease caused by the radiation," she said. "I am very ill." I don't recall knowing exactly what was wrong with her, but she was healed when I touched her. She continued, "And my child is deformed, also caused by the fallout of the radiation." I saw the little girl's hands were deformed.

Again I responded, "But that's no problem for the Lord, either." I reached out, touched the little girl and asked the Lord to heal her. She was given a creative miracle, and her hands became normal. The people were astounded, as anyone would be, but in the vision I was not. I fully expected God to heal and deliver the people.

I then said to all of them, "Come on, let's go get in the river."

"Oh, no," they replied, "the water is polluted."

"Not this water," I said smiling, and I led them into the river behind me.

Messy and Undignified—and Loving It!

Again, the Lord said to me, "Let's go."

"Where?" I asked.

"You'll see," He again responded, and off we went once more. This time we landed on a beach. It was similar to a public beach with places to play, relax or rest.

"What are we doing here?" I inquired.

"It's time for some rest and relaxation," He replied.

"But who will go to all the other places and tell them the good news?" I asked Him.

"Oh, I have lots of others who'll go," He responded. "It's time for you to rest."

At this point, my wife, Ceci, and our two daughters, Sarah and Hannah, came walking towards me. The girls and the Lord went to the water and began to play—yes, He frolicked with them, too—while Ceci and I lay on the beach resting. A few minutes later, Jesus came toward me carrying something. As He came

———

It was messy and undignified, and Jesus was loving it. He loved to shock me with His humor and lightheartedness.

———

closer, I could see it was a birthday cake. (This vision actually occurred the day before my birthday.)

"Happy birthday," He said, extending the cake my way.

"Wow, Lord!" was my surprised exclamation. "I can't believe you got me a birthday cake!"

"Sure," He said. "Let's celebrate."

"Go ahead and cut it then," I suggested.

"*Cut* it?!" He replied in sort of a comical and teasing manner. "We're not gonna cut it." (Listen, when Jesus talks to someone in Mexico, He speaks Spanish. When in France, He speaks French. When He spoke to this Texan, He said "gonna"!) He then began breaking off pieces by hand and passing them out to my family. It was messy and undignified, and Jesus was loving it. It seemed He loved to shock me with His humor and lightheartedness. By the way, it was carrot cake—my favorite.

"Loosen Up!"

At this point the vision ended, and I found myself on the floor in front of the podium. Several people were there milling around, the service having ended. I had lain there 45 minutes. I was told I wept one minute and laughed the next. This came as no surprise to me because Jesus and I went from frolicking and fun to reaching the unreached, from healing the sick to fun again. I laughed and cried in the vision as well. It was quite a ride and quite a swim!

You may think my vision strange, but the Bible is filled with unusual visions, from Daniel's beasts (see Dan. 8) to Peter's sheet-wrapped animals (see Acts 10) to Ezekiel's own vision of the river (see Ezek. 47). To stay free of error, we must judge a vision by Scripture and allow it to speak that which God intends without glorifying it or creating doctrine from it.

Don Crum, a minister visiting our church that weekend who has a strong prophetic anointing, thought the cake scene was especially meaningful. "You always want things just right, Dutch," he told me. "Everything in order, sliced neatly, perfect. But God is saying, 'Loosen up, chill out. Don't expect everything to be so perfect.' God's not always going to *cut* the cake."

That very week, Barbara Blake, a dear friend of ours and an intercessor in our fellowship, handed me the most recent edition of Every Home for Christ's monthly magazine. The issue hadn't yet been publicly released. On the cover in large, bold letters was the word "Chernobyl." This was confirmation to me that the vision was indeed from the Lord (not that I needed one) and that God was literally going to send me to Chernobyl.

The Great Thirst Quencher

I am certainly not unique as one who has experienced God's river. Many others today have been in His river—some seeing visions, most probably not. But thousands of people have been, and continue to be, changed through an outpouring of the Holy Spirit many are simply calling "the river of God."

This book and my vision are about much more than a river, however. They are about a Person. The river flows *from God.* It is His life flowing forth.

And he showed me a river of the water of life, clear as crystal, coming from the throne of God and *of the Lamb* (Rev. 22:1, italics mine).

He who believes in Me, as the Scripture said, "From his

innermost being shall flow rivers of living water." But this *He spoke of the Spirit*, whom those who believed in Him were to receive; for the Spirit was not yet given, because Jesus was not yet glorified" (John 7:38,39, italics mine).

They drink their fill of the abundance of Thy house; and Thou dost give them to drink of the river of Thy delights. For *with Thee* is the fountain of life; in Thy light we see light (Ps. 36:8,9, italics mine).

Numerous other references could be given, but the point is clearly made. When we speak of the river of God, we're not referring to a place, a thing or an experience; we're referring to the very life of God. The river and other references to life-giving water in the Scriptures represent the life that flows out from God.

- To be in the river is to be in God.
- To drink from the river is to drink from God.
- To release the river is to release God.

―

As humans, we thrive on and crave experiences.
God is often lost in our search for God!

―

In the vision I shared with you, I wasn't captivated by the river itself or the water—I was captivated by Jesus.

As humans, we thrive on and crave experiences. We want to see and feel. In this pursuit, we are driven to endless activities and surface relationships. Our pursuit of God can deteriorate into the pursuit of one spiritual high after another. *God is often lost in our search for God!* Even those of us in full-time Christian ministry are prone to run from one ministry experience to another.

But the story of the Bible isn't God and activity or God and His experiences. The Bible is not about God and things, and it's certainly not about God and religion. The story of the Bible is God and people. The story of the Cross is God reunited with people. *He is all about experiencing relationship.* And any spiritual experience that does not in some way draw us closer to Him has either been wasted or wasn't from God at all.

As you and I begin this book journey by focusing on the other facets of the river—its many symbolic uses in Scripture, the pictures and lessons revealed, even the fruit or effect produced—we run the risk of perverting this truth. While we will study these things, we want to see them in their proper context—Christ. His life, His fullness, His attributes.

We have no need for more Marthas who let service *get in the way of* relationship (see Luke 10:38-42).

We want no more Jonahs who have service, but *no* relationship (see Jon. 1,2).

We must guard against the deception of the Ephesians who let service *take the place of* relationship (see Rev. 2:2-4).

We dare not make the mistake of Saul who *mistook religious activity and sacrifice* for relationship (see 1 Sam. 15:1-23).

All these men and women experienced the river, but allowed it to become polluted by misplaced priorities through the deception of the enemy.

River experiences, even revival, can be allowed to replace *Him*. One way to lose a move of God is to lose God in the move. This has happened in almost every former awakening or season of revival. We must guard against this subtle snare as we would the plague.

During our journey through these pages together, my prayer is that you will be motivated to go to Him and drink. Not to a meeting, a revival or a minister, which can all be good, but to Him.

He, Jesus, is the Great Thirst Quencher!

Note
1. Quoted from my brother, Pastor Tim Sheets.

CHAPTER TWO

The Cross:
Where the River Begins

A few years ago at the Seattle Special Olympics, nine contestants, all physically or mentally disabled, assembled at the starting line for the 100-yard dash. At the gun they all started out, not exactly in a dash, but with the relish to run the race to the finish and win.

All, that is, except one boy who stumbled on the asphalt, tumbled over a couple of times, and began to cry. The other eight heard the boy cry. They slowed down and paused. Then they all turned around and went back. Every one of them. One girl with Down's syndrome bent down and kissed him and said, "This will make it better." Then all nine linked arms and walked together to the finish line.

Everyone in the stadium stood, and the cheering went on for 10 minutes.[1]

At the Cross, God picked us up and said, "This will make you feel better. Let's link arms and walk to the finish line together."

There is a powerful, cleansing, thirst-quenching river that flows from the Cross even today. Let's link arms and jump in! You'll feel better.

Beautiful, Terrifying Waters

God likes water. He talks a lot about it in His Word and often compares Himself and His attributes to the properties of water. He used to take walks on it. A river actually flows from His throne.

The Lord begins speaking about rivers in the second chapter of Genesis and doesn't finish until the last chapter of Revelation—and says a lot of interesting and powerful things in between.

- He compares the life in Him (which ultimately becomes the life in us) to water, calling it a well, a fountain, a stream, a river and rain.
- He uses peaceful water to paint a picture of the rest He desires to give us (see Ps. 23:2).
- He mentions the river of delights and "a river whose streams make glad the city of God" (Ps. 46:4).
- He speaks of the passion of love using such phrases as "a garden spring," "a well of fresh water" and "streams flowing from Lebanon" (Song of Sol. 4:15).
- He even compares His Word to water (see Eph. 5:26).

A person has only to sit by a mountain stream for an hour or two to realize how special and therapeutic water can be. Have you ever de-stressed on a beach early in the morning or late at night, listening to the waves endlessly lapping at the shore? I recently stood at Niagara Falls and was overwhelmed by its majesty. It was at once beautiful and terrifying. This paradox reminded me of the description of God in Exodus 15:11, "fearful in praises, doing wonders" (*KJV*).

Several years ago, I visited Victoria Falls in Zimbabwe, Africa. One of the seven natural wonders of the world, it is awe-inspiring beyond description. So much spray rose above it that, from a distance, it looked as though a cloud were hovering there. Rainbows were everywhere. As I soaked in its grandeur, I thought of the verse, "His voice was like the sound of many waters" (Rev. 1:15). It is little wonder the Israelites were terrified when He spoke from the mountain (see Exod. 20:18,19). I think I, too, prefer the still, small voice.

There is just something special about water. Life can't exist without it. Did you know the human body is 65% water? You're all wet!

Name That Revival

Why all the talk today about "the river"? Is it coincidental? It seems every season of renewal or revival takes on a name. Whether it's the Protestant reformation, the charismatic renewal or the Jesus movement, we label them. The current move of the Holy Spirit around the world is being referred to by many as "the river." Why?

I certainly wouldn't suggest God has named all these movements, but the names do often characterize certain truths, doctrines or works of the Spirit associated with them.

Why is this current movement being spoken of so often and by so many in connection with the river of God? Is there any real biblical significance to this? Could the Holy Spirit be making this association? If so, how do the rivers in Scripture relate to the moving of the Holy Spirit today? What are the symbolic meanings and truths we need to understand?

Though I believe this linking is of the Holy Spirit, please know my purpose for this book is not to name a revival. Isn't that just what we need—another label in the Body of Christ to further distinguish ourselves from one another? "I'm an evangelical." "I'm a charismatic." "I'm a riverite."

Herman Ostry's barn floor was under 29 inches of water because of a rising creek. The Bruno, Nebraska, farmer invited a few friends to a barn raising. He needed to move his entire 17,000-pound barn to a new foundation more than 143 feet away. His son, Mike, devised a latticework of steel tubing, and nailed, bolted and welded it on the inside and the outside of the barn. Hundreds of handles were attached.

After one practice lift, 344 volunteers slowly walked the barn up a slight incline, each supporting less than fifty pounds. In just three minutes, the barn was on its new foundation.

The Body of Christ can accomplish great things when we work together.[2]

Forget the labels, let's just get the barn moved! As someone once said, "None of us is as smart as all of us."[3]

No, I'm not writing a book to name this revival. But I do wish to reveal the significance of this present move of the Holy Spirit being compared to a river. I want to look at the river of God in Scripture to glean the powerful truths hidden there. The principles discussed will be pertinent to any season of revival or move of the Holy Spirit.

Water and Power Company

As I said before, the river of God in Scripture represents His life and power. At times the water flows from Christ; at other times the flow is attributed to the Holy Spirit. It is safe to say Christ is the source of the water of life, and the Holy Spirit causes it to flow, or distributes it. The important thing to know, however, is that the river represents spiritual life and power—God's life.

Respected teacher and author Fuchsia Pickett tells of a vision she was given by the Holy Spirit in 1963. In this detailed vision, which lasted for two days, the Lord used the analogy of a hydroelectric power plant to show her the revival that was coming to the Church.

The vision came in such detail that the head engineer of the Pacific Power Company in Oregon couldn't believe the details came from Dr. Pickett. "This paper is one of the most scientific I have ever read," he stated. "There are words and terms in here that only a few master electricians know and understand."[4]

Dr. Pickett saw the power plant constructed: its pipes, the dam, prime lines, transformers and many other details. The power plant represented the Church Christ was building and the awe-some power of the Holy Spirit that would flow from it. She says:

> When God releases His *dunamis* power in this next move of God, rivers of living water will flow out of our innermost beings. Habakkuk's prophecy will become a reality: "For the earth shall be filled with the knowledge of the glory of the Lord, as the waters cover the sea" (Hab. 2:14, *NKJV*).
>
> At the time of my vision, my Father said to me, "I am running the pipes now. And this time when I pull that great power switch and release all the rivers of my living Word in their fullness, no demon, devil, man or denomination will ever dam it up again. I will do a quick work; I am going to bring the revival that will result in the ingathering of the great harvest of souls."[5]

The river is being released and will, in its fullness, result in the greatest harvest the earth has ever known. It will be glorious!

Dr. Pickett believes the current move of the Holy Spirit around the world is the beginning of this vision's fulfillment. I agree. The river is being released and will, in its fullness, result in the greatest harvest the earth has ever known. It will be glorious!

There Is a Fountain
Water is seen in Scripture in various forms—rivers, streams, brooks, rain, clouds, vapor, dew, wells, fountains. It is not the form that matters. The focus is not on the channel of a stream or river, but on the water itself. Likewise, in our study of the river of God we must remember and focus on what it represents, regardless of the analogy used.

Numerous spiritual truths are illustrated in Scripture by water, such as God's life, God's power, His glory, blessings, revival, the Word of God, cleansing, judgment, death and burial of the old sinful nature (water baptism), the human race, direction and praise.

Many scriptural references to water represent spiritual life. In studying these, one truth emerges as critical and perhaps the most encompassing: The water flows *from Christ* and was *released at the Cross*. He is the source. *The headwaters are found in Him.*

Revelation 22:1,2 makes this clear:

And he showed me a river of the water of life, clear as crystal, *coming from the throne of God and of the Lamb,* in the middle of its street. And on either side of the river was the tree of life, bearing twelve kinds of fruit, yielding its fruit every month; and the leaves of the tree were for the healing of the nations (italics mine).

The source of the river was pictured for us in a vivid way when Christ was crucified. From His side flowed "blood *and water*" (John 19:34). Yes, it looked like a trickle, but it was a river that has since quenched the thirst of millions. Truly, He is the fountain of life.

All the drink offerings in the Old Testament anticipated this life being poured from Christ (see Gen. 35:14 and Exod. 29:40,41 as examples). The pouring of water onto the ground was symbolic of what would take place at the Cross. A great story from the life of King David vividly demonstrates this. During a battle with the Philistines, David was homesick and had a craving for a drink from the well of Bethlehem (see 1 Chron. 11:15-19). Three of his mighty men broke through the Philistine camp, drew water from the well, and carried it to David.

The water, however, was too precious for David to consume himself. Instead, he decided to pour it out as an offering to the Lord. What a picture! Though unknown to David, this drink offering represented the pouring out of *the* Drink Offering, God's well of salvation born in Bethlehem. Those watching

David's drink offering were staring (probably in disbelief) at a sacrifice that foretold the greatest event in history—Christ's sacrifice on the cross, where humankind's thirst was satisfied.

Just as David's homesickness led him to the well, ours leads us to the Cross where we, too, find the thirst-quenching flow.

One of the reference points of London is the Charing Cross. It is near the geographical center of the city and serves as a navigational tool for those confused by the streets.

A little girl was lost in the great city. A policeman found her. Between sobs and tears, she explained she didn't know her way home. He asked her if she knew her address. She didn't. He asked her phone number; she didn't know that either. But when he asked her what she knew, suddenly her face lit up.

"I know the Cross," she said, "show me the Cross and I can find my way home from there."[6]

The Cross has been leading us home for 2,000 years.

Another great picture associating the Cross with water is found in Exodus 17:1-7. Israel was without water in the wilderness, but God supplied it for them from a rock.

Then the Lord said to Moses, "Pass before the people and take with you some of the elders of Israel; and take in your hand your staff with which you struck the Nile, and go. Behold, I will stand before you there on the rock at Horeb; and you shall strike the rock, and water will come out of it, that the people may drink." And Moses did so in the sight of the elders of Israel (Exod. 17:5,6).

Psalms tells us this water gushed like a river.

He split the rocks in the wilderness, and gave them abundant drink like the ocean depths. He brought forth streams also from the rock, and caused waters to run down like

rivers. May He send you help from the sanctuary, and support you from Zion! (Ps. 78:15,16; 20:2).

First Corinthians 10:4 tells us, "And all drank the same spiritual drink, for they were drinking from a spiritual rock which followed them; and the rock was Christ." This rock from which the

---

God came and cried with us at the Cross.
He was there for us. He shouted the cry of
every human who has ever lived: "I thirst!"

---

river flowed was a type or picture of Christ being smitten on the
cross, bringing forth the water of life. In fact, the Hebrew word
for Moses striking the rock (see Exod. 17:6), and Christ being
smitten (see Isa. 53:4) are actually the same, *nakah*. When the
Rock, Christ Jesus, was smitten, a river flowed to the human race.
He who cried on the cross, "I thirst" (John 19:28) was taking on
the craving of humanity. Who can comprehend such a thing? The
Fountain of living water Himself was thirsty. The angels must
have been speechless with confusion and awe.

Author and lecturer Leo Buscaglia once talked about a
contest he was asked to judge. The purpose of the contest
was to find the most caring child. The winner was a four-
year-old child whose next-door neighbor was an elderly
gentleman who had recently lost his wife. Upon seeing the
man cry, the little boy went into the old gentleman's yard,
climbed onto his lap and just sat there. When his mother
asked him what he had said to the neighbor, the little boy
said, "Nothing, I just helped him cry."[7]

God came and cried with us at the Cross. He was there for us.
He shouted the cry of every human who has ever lived: "I thirst!"

And in the most amazing act of mercy and love the world has witnessed, God opened the fountain of life—Moses' rock was smitten—and water flowed in the desert. Jesus must have been thinking of this when He said to the thirsty adulteress, "Whoever drinks of the water that I shall give him shall never thirst" (John 4:14).

Choose a Man

The word *nakah* appears in yet another passage which depicts the Cross. In 1 Samuel 17:49, the word is used to describe the rock from David's sling "striking" Goliath on the forehead. It is not coincidental that David used a *rock* taken from a *brook* to kill the giant. This is a wonderful picture of Christ, the "*rock* of our salvation" (Ps. 95:1), the "chief corner *stone*" (Ps. 118:22), the brook-producing Rock Himself, crushing the head of Satan (see Gen. 3:15).

41

Follow this progression. Goliath was the greatest of all the giants, the champion. One translation calls him the "shocktrooper."[8] He was so huge it was shocking. He represents Satan, the greatest enemy of God and man. David represents Christ, the "son of David." In this passage from 1 Samuel, we see a prophetic drama foreshadowing the most pivotal event in the history of the human race. "Choose a man," Goliath/Satan challenged. "If he is able to fight with me and kill me, then we will become your servants; but if I prevail against him and kill him, then you shall become our servants and serve us" (1 Sam. 17:8,9).

The dilemma of humankind is depicted here by Israel. In the war with Satan, which began in the garden of Eden, our freedom hung in the balance. The challenge was issued by the serpent to the human race, "I have defeated you and made you serve me. You will be my slaves, unless you can find a human capable of conquering me."

"Choose a man," Goliath sneered for 40 days and nights—80 times.

"Choose a man," Satan mocked for 4,000 years, while creation reeled under his onslaught.

Listen to Isaiah describe the scene:

And justice is turned back, and righteousness stands far away; for truth has stumbled in the street, and uprightness cannot enter. Yes, truth is lacking; and he who turns aside from evil makes himself a prey. Now the Lord saw, and it was displeasing in His sight that there was no justice. And He saw that there was *no man,* and was astonished that there was no one to intercede (Isa. 59:14-16, italics mine).

But God had a plan. His Champion was waiting in heaven. The great Shepherd, the son of shepherd David, was listening to the taunts, biding His time. When it was right, God packaged eternity into a microscopic seed and planted it in the womb of a virgin.

The Creator entered creation.

The all-powerful God of thunder and light—He who shakes mountains when He speaks, indeed He who creates solar systems with a word, *He who kicked Satan out of heaven with one brilliant flash of His glory*—entered the battlefield. A qualified (He was human), sufficient (He was God) challenger arrived in Bethlehem, the birthplace of His predecessor, David.

Angels sang, shepherds worshiped (Satan must hate shepherds—talk about painful memories!), the Holy Spirit hovered and the Father smiled. "I have chosen a Man," He whispered with a smile. Then He chuckled...just before He roared.

You don't think so? Listen to Psalm 2:4,7,8. "He who sits in the heavens *laughs*....I will surely tell of the decree of the Lord: He said to Me, 'Thou art My Son, today I have begotten Thee. Ask of Me, and I will surely give the nations as Thine inheritance, and the very ends of the earth as Thy possession'" (italics mine).

Hell must have been confused, terrified and furious. How could this be? Damage control would probably be a fair description of the board meeting in the netherworld. This was not what was expected.

Back to the scene in Israel. Goliath had challenged Israel for 40 days and nights. Forty is the biblical number of testing, and Israel's courage and trust in God were being tested. More than a thousand years after this encounter, Jesus would have two major meetings with Satan, one of them coming after *40* days of fasting when He was tested by the devil in the wilderness. He, as David, finished off His adversary with a sword—the sword of the Spirit. "It is written," He said.

His other major confrontation with Satan would take place at the Cross, also pictured by this battle between David and Goliath. Before meeting Goliath, David went to a brook and gathered *five* stones. The Amplified translation says David put them in his "lunch bag" (1 Sam. 17:40). He intended to have Goliath for lunch! This was going to be a picnic. How's *that* for faith?

The number five in Scripture represents the Cross, grace, atonement and life.[9] There were five sacrificial offerings—the burnt sacrifice, the grain offering, the peace offering, the sin offering and the trespass offering—established by God in

—

When Christ was smitten, the river of life
flowed, and the headship or dominion
of the serpent was ended. Hallelujah!

—

Leviticus 1-7, all picturing the *Cross*, where God's *grace* was poured out, giving us *life*. Five wounds were inflicted on Jesus at the Cross—His hands, feet and side. Numerous other examples could be given to illustrate the consistency of this application.

David went to the brook, probably got a good long drink, and picked up the five *stones* representing Christ our *Rock*, the Cross and the grace of God. He flung one stone into the head of Goliath. In fulfillment, Christ our Rock, the chief Corner*stone* and the Son of David, smote the head of the biggest giant, the serpent. He is THE Rock, THE chief Stone—our great, human, shepherding, giant-killing Hero!

Thus, in Moses and David we have two smitings, each picturing different facets of the same event. When Moses' rock was smitten (*nakah*) the river flowed. When David flung the rock, striking (*nakah*) Goliath's head, the enemy was defeated. When Christ was smitten (*nakah*) the river of life flowed, and the headship or dominion of the serpent was ended. Hallelujah!

Psalm 110 prophesied this crushing the head of the enemy. "Head" is translated from the Hebrew word *rosh*, which means headship or authority. Verse six states Christ would shatter the *rosh* (headship) over the *erets* (earth). Then verse seven predicts He would become the new *rosh*. The first part of this seventh verse declares—notice the similarity to David—"He will drink from the brook by the wayside." Moffat translates it, "He drinks from any stream he has to cross, then charges forward triumphing." The Amplified says, "He will drink of the brook by the way; therefore will He lift up His head triumphantly."

I don't suppose I can prove it, but I like to think this is in keeping with the picture we just described. David went to the brook, took a big drink, grabbed the five stones and ran to meet Goliath. Jesus, the Son of David, took a big drink from the river of life in heaven—maybe even a literal one from the brook Kidron next to Gethsemane—and charged forth triumphing.

Can God ever write a script!

Crossing the River into the Promised Land

Before we move on to other truths pictured by water in Scripture, let's briefly look at three more biblical water paintings of the Cross.

In Exodus 15:22-26, the Israelites were in the wilderness of Shur and could find no water. They came to a place called Marah, meaning "bitterness." There was water; but as the name would indicate, it was too bitter to drink. God showed Moses a tree that upon being thrown into the waters, purified them.

This is undoubtedly a picture of the Cross, healing the bitter waters of sin in the human race. God even established one of His redemptive names at this event, Jehovah Ropheka, which means "the Lord your Healer." The Cross, of course, is where this name found its ultimate fulfillment.

The other two biblical water paintings picturing the Cross are Christ's baptism and Joshua leading the Israelites across the Jordan River into Canaan. Not only do both events picture the Cross, but both also involve water baptism.

Jesus' baptism in the Jordan River by John (see Matt. 3:13-17) is a picture of Christ's death and burial. Going under the water represents burial, and rising from the water symbolizes resurrection.

Christ's baptism and what it represents—the Cross—were powerfully pictured by Joshua and Israel in Joshua 3 when they crossed the Jordan River into the Promised Land. Crossing the Jordan represented moving from death to life—from the Cross to resurrection.

The Jordan River dividing the wilderness and Canaan represents death—the death of the old sinful man. This is also seen in Christ's baptism in the Jordan—symbolizing His baptism into death. As a further illustration, the Jordan River actually flows into the Dead Sea, place of the lowest elevation on earth where nothing can live.

The Waters of Death Rolled Back
At the time of the crossing, the Jordan River was in flood stage (see Josh. 3:15) which made it totally impassable for Israel. In their own abilities, they could not cross it, just as it is impossible for us in our own strength to move from spiritual death to life.

Joshua was given the key. He was told to first send the Ark of the Covenant into the water. The Ark, with the blood-sprinkled mercy seat on top, pictures the shedding of Christ's blood on the cross. Joshua 3:11 states literally, "Behold, the Ark of the Covenant, the Lord of all the earth is crossing over ahead of you into the Jordan."[10] Surely this is a picture of Christ entering into death for us.

Verses 15 and 16 tell us when "the feet of the priests carrying the ark were dipped in the edge of the water," the waters rolled back. "Dipped" is the Old Testament word for baptism. The meaning is very clear, just as it is with Christ's baptism: When Christ was dipped—baptized—into death, the power of death was rolled back.

Incredibly, the river was rolled back to a small town named Adam, miles upstream (see Josh. 3:16). Could this be a coincidence? Never! As a picture for us of what Jesus, our Joshua, was going to do, God rolled the Jordan River all the way back to Adam. In fulfillment, Jesus cut off the waters of death flowing into the "dead sea" of humanity all the way back to the fall of Adam. What an amazing picture! The Cross shut off the flow of one river—death—while releasing another—life! The impossible doesn't exist with Him. When dealing with God, "I have learned to use the word 'impossible' with the greatest caution."[11]

The priests were told to remain in the dry riverbed with the Ark until all Israel had crossed. This is a picture of us being "crucified with Christ" (Gal. 2:20). Water baptism, of course, signifies this for the believer.

Finally, Israel was told to build two memorials, one in the Jordan riverbed (which pictures the Cross) and one in the Promised Land (which pictures the Resurrection). Interestingly, explicit instructions were given that the resurrection memorial had to be made out of stones taken *from the Jordan riverbed.* Why? To picture for us that the only way to life—resurrection— is through the Cross. The only way to live is to die with Christ. No Cross (death of the old), no resurrection (new life).

A "believe-it-or-not" picture showed a tomb with a fig tree growing out of the middle of it; the tree split the great slab of stone that formed the top of the sarcophagus into three great pieces, and pushed out the side walls with the force of its growth. The tomb, it is said, is in the grounds of the parish church of Watford, England, and is that of a naval officer, Ben Wangford, whose dying request was that he might be buried with a fig in his hand. The life of that fig took hold of the death of that hand and the power of the life split the tomb.[12]

Christ entered death for us and with Him carried a seed from the tree of life. The life of that seed took hold of the death of that hand and split the tomb with His resurrection life. "Death is swallowed up in victory. O death, where is your victory? O death, where is your sting?" (1 Cor. 15:54,55).

Our study of the river of God all begins here at the Cross. The river of death stops, and the river of life initiates there. All other river revelations fade in comparison to this. At the Cross, the river of God's life cascaded into the abyss of death and rendered it powerless. It plunged into the depths of sin and cleansed its defilement.

In the words of the great hymn:

> There is a fountain filled with blood
>> Drawn from Emmanuel's veins,
> And sinners plunged beneath that flood
>> Lose all their guilty stains.[13]

Notes

1. Jack Canfield and Mark Victor Hansen, *A Third Serving of Chicken Soup for the Soul* (Deerfield Beach, FL: Health Communications, Inc., 1996), p. 70.
2. Edward K. Rowell, *Fresh Illustrations for Preaching and Teaching* (Grand Rapids: Baker Books, 1997), p. 205.
3. Edward K. Rowell, *Quotes & Idea Starters for Preaching and Teaching* (Grand Rapids: Baker Books, 1996), p. 163.
4. Fuchsia Pickett, *The Next Move of God* (Lake Mary, FL: Creation House, 1994), p. 13.
5. Ibid., pp. 12, 13.
6. Max Lucado, *And the Angels Were Silent* (Portland: Multnomah Press, 1992), p. 43.
7. Canfield, *A Third Serving of Chicken Soup for the Soul*, p. 12.
8. *Twenty Six Translations of the Bible* (Atlanta: Mathis Publishers, 1985), p. 939.
9. Kevin Conner, *The Tabernacle of Moses* (Portland: Bible Temple Publications, 1974), p. 146.
10. *New Geneva Study Bible* (Foundation for Reformation, Thomas Nelson Publishers, 1995).
11. Canfield, *A Third Serving of Chicken Soup for the Soul*, p. 299.
12. Donald Grey Barnhouse, *Let Me Illustrate* (Grand Rapids: Fleming H. Revell, 1967), pp. 140, 141.
13. William Cowper, traditional American melody, "There Is a Fountain."

CHAPTER THREE

The Harvest River

Soon after her brother was born, little Sachi began to ask her parents to leave her alone with the new baby. They worried that like most four-year-olds, she might feel jealous and want to hit or shake him, so they said no. But she showed no signs of jealousy. She treated the baby with kindness, and her pleas to be left alone with him became more urgent. They decided to allow it.

Elated, she went into the baby's room and shut the door, but it opened a crack—enough for her curious parents to peek in and listen. They saw little Sachi walk quietly up to her baby brother, put her face close to his and say quietly, "Baby, tell me what God looks like. I'm starting to forget."[1]

Christ came to show us what God looked like. Humankind had forgotten. Sin, Satan, even religion had erased the memory from our souls. John 1:18 tells us Jesus came to "explain" God. The Greek word for "explain" is *exegeomai*, from which the word exegete is derived.

Jesus exegeted God for us. Characteristic by characteristic, heartbeat by heartbeat, miracle by miracle, teaching by teaching, Christ revealed God.

A few chapters later in John 7:37-39, Jesus dissected some religious tradition and showed us the face of God.

Now on the last day, the great day of the feast, Jesus stood and cried out, saying, "If any man is thirsty, let him come to Me and drink. He who believes in Me, as the Scripture said, 'From his innermost being shall flow *rivers* of living water.'" But this He spoke of the Spirit, whom those who believed in Him were to receive; for the Spirit was not yet given, because Jesus was not yet glorified.

Incredibly, at least six important truths are hidden in these three verses. (Many more if we were to count all the things pictured by the Feast of Tabernacles, the feast mentioned in the passage.) These are:

1. The Cross, where Christ was later poured out and became to us the fountain of life;
2. The pouring out of the Holy Spirit at Pentecost;
3. Seasons of great spiritual harvest;
4. We, the Body of Christ, becoming the temple of the Holy Spirit;
5. The Holy Spirit flowing from us like a river;
6. Our need to continually drink of Him in order to experience the continual flow of the river.

Let's look at these verses and feast on the riches found there.

The Feast of Tabernacles

First of all, the timing of this great declaration is mentioned and is important to know. It was "the last day, the great day of the feast." As I already stated, the feast spoken of here is the Feast of Tabernacles.

Three main feasts were annual events among the Israelites: Passover, Pentecost and Tabernacles. These feasts coincided with and represented two *harvest* periods (grain; oil and wine) and two corresponding seasons of *rain* (early; latter). Both rainy seasons were essential—one for each period of harvest—if the growing seasons were to be successful.

The first two feasts, Passover and Pentecost, were associated with the grain harvest and the latter rains. Because Passover anticipated the Cross, and Pentecost signaled the outpouring of the Holy Spirit recorded in Acts 2, many believe the grain harvest associated with them represents the *first great ingathering of souls*, which took place in the book of Acts. The rain associated with this physical harvest season is a picture of the outpouring of the Holy Spirit. Joel prophesied, "I will pour out my Spirit on all mankind" (Joel 2:28). Peter said at Pentecost, "This is what was spoken of through the prophet Joel" (Acts 2:16).

The last of the three feasts, Tabernacles, was associated with the wine and oil harvest and linked to the early rains. It was also called the Feast of Ingathering, because it represented the final great harvest of the year. If it had been a good year of reaping, this was an especially joyful time of celebration. People were thankful, relieved and ready for some rest.

Double Harvest
Together, Israel's three major feasts picture the Cross, the outpouring of the Holy Spirit and great seasons of spiritual harvest. An amazing prophecy in Joel declares there is a day coming when God is going to combine these seasons into a period of great spiritual harvest.

> So rejoice, O sons of Zion, and be glad in the Lord your God; for He has given you the early rain for your vindication. And He has poured down for you the rain, *the early and latter rain* as before. And the threshing floors will be full of grain, and the vats will overflow with the new wine and oil (Joel 2:23,24, italics mine).

Using these two harvest periods and the two rainy seasons associated with them, the Lord said one day there will come such a tremendous spiritual reaping that it will be as a combination of two harvests. When this occurs "the threshing floors will be full" and "the vats will overflow." The ingathering will be so great there will not be room enough to contain it.

Amos, in his prophecy, states it this way: "The plowman will overtake the reaper and the treader of grapes him who sows seed"

—

> The greatest Farmer the world has
> ever known is pursuing the greatest
> harvest the world has ever seen!

—

(Amos 9:13). In other words, there will be so much to glean that when it is time to plow and sow again for the next crop, the reapers will not yet have been able to bring in all the previous harvest.

Are we moving into a time such as this? Many, including myself, believe we are coming into this double harvest. Though America is not yet experiencing its fruit, the harvest has already begun in other nations. Approximately 178,000 people are being born again throughout the world each day.[2] This is three times the natural birthrate! For the first time in history, we are gaining on the earth's population.

The *greatest Farmer* the world has ever known is pursuing the *greatest harvest* the world has ever seen! The Lord of the harvest is doing some Lording!

- He *will* see the fruit of His labor and be satisfied (see Isa. 53:11).
- He *is* bringing many sons to glory (see Heb. 2:10).
- The threshing floors *will* be full; the vats *will* overflow (see Joel 2:24).
- The plowman *will* overtake the reaper (see Amos 9:13).
- The estimated 8,000 unreached people groups *will* be reached.

- The one billion Muslims of the world *will* be impacted.
- The 800 million Hindus of India *will* hear.
- Men from *every* tribe and tongue and people and nation *will* be among the worshipers of the Lamb (see Rev. 7:9).

When this heavenly sickle is released with its full force, no place will be safe from its reach!

We are the generation of believers with the incredible privilege of reaping the greatest harvest of souls into the kingdom of God since the Cross. Actually more than all other generations combined. It's bumper crop time!

The Great Day of the Feast

The first thing, then, significant about Christ's words in John 7 is *Jesus picked a time that represented a great harvest season to make this declaration about the river of living waters.* Don't think for a second this could be coincidental.

In His wisdom, not only did He choose this feast to make his proclamation, but He chose the last day of the feast, commonly referred to as "the great day." An important ritual took place at this time called "the outpouring of the waters." On this day water was taken from Siloam and poured on the altar while Isaiah 12:3 was quoted, "Therefore you will joyously draw water from the springs of salvation."

Follow the symbolism carefully—believe me it's worth the brain energy you will expend. Siloam means "sent" (see John 9:7) and the water from this pool came primarily from Gihon Spring, located outside the city. Gihon means "bursting forth."

It is believed Jesus picked this moment when the water from Siloam—which came from Gihon, outside the city—was being poured out, and Isaiah 12:3 was being quoted, to make this declaration. Picture the scene. The city was crowded during this festive and joyous occasion. Thousands of people were celebrating a successful harvest. At a climatic moment in the celebration, Jesus interrupted the tradition, declaring in essence, "Hey, everyone!

Look over here. I am Siloam, *sent* by the Father. I will be crucified *outside the city*. I am *the spring* of salvation. From My side, blood and water will *burst forth* (Gihon) and be poured onto the earth. I am the Drink Offering. If any man is thirsty, let him come to Me and drink." Wow!

No, those in attendance didn't realize or comprehend all this, but we should. And whether they understood or not, you can be certain He got their attention.

To further enhance the picture for us, a few days later Jesus performed another act which probably no one understood at the time. He made clay out of spittle and applied it to a blind man's eyes (see John 9:6). He then told him to go wash in the pool of Siloam. The man went, washed and came back seeing. This demonstrated for us the fact that He, the *sent One* from the Father, came to wash us and open our blind eyes. He will remove the darkness and bring light. This Feast of Tabernacles was actually also called the Feast of Illumination. So much light was associated with it, historian Alfred Edersheim says, "There was not a court in Jerusalem that was not lit up by the light."[3]

When Jesus chose this day and time to make His announcement, He was stating emphatically that *the spring of salvation would flow from Him, the sent One, causing the great spiritual harvest pictured by this feast.*

Don't you just love it when the Lord takes dead religion, often paralyzed by powerless tradition or seemingly meaningless ritual, and infuses it with life? Religion in its pure sense is good; but if powered only by forms and rituals, it can be anemic to its owner and disgusting to those around it. As John Bunyan so accurately stated, "Religion is the best armor a man can have, but it is the worst cloak."[4]

William Poteet wrote in *The Pentecostal Minister* how in 1903 the Russian czar noticed a sentry posted for no apparent reason on the Kremlin grounds. Upon inquiry, he discovered that in 1776 Catherine the Great found there the

first flower of spring. "Post a sentry here," she commanded, "so that no one tramples that flower under foot!"

Some traditions die hard.[5]

Through the present renewal, God is doing for us what He did
for these Jews in the Temple. He is life-ing our anemic religious
activity. He is sending (Siloam) His living water, causing it to burst
forth (Gihon) in our midst causing the river of His Spirit to flow.

Bring it on Lord—we're thirsty! And give us the grace to
change whatever is necessary for us to receive it.

—

> In a humanistic world of amorality and
> perversion, people are looking for a
> demonstration of true character and integrity.

55

—

Those in the world are also thirsty. Don't let them fool you
with their seeming disinterest. They simply haven't been satisfied
with our stained glass placebos. They are crying out for *substance*.

A Hungry, Thirsty World

In a humanistic world of amorality and perversion, people are
looking for a demonstration of true character and integrity. A
world, screaming out one side of its mouth that it doesn't
believe in absolutes, desperately wants some. A dog-eat-dog
society with greed as its basic motivation is begging to see some
true *agape*. Consider these alarming facts:

- More than 3 million crimes occur on or near school
  campuses every year.
- One in five high school students carries a weapon.
- One in 20 high school students carries a gun.
- During our century, the divorce rate has risen 700
  percent.

- Thirteen million children under the age of 18 are grow-ing up with one or both parents away from home.
- Seventy percent of all juveniles in state reform institu-tions come from fatherless homes.
- By 1994 more than 30 million babies in America had been aborted. (The most recent figure is 35 million.)
- The U.S. is the single greatest market on the globe for illegal drugs and leads the world in the export of pornography.
- Even with all our well-meaning legislation and social reform programs, the '90s have seen polarization between races in the U.S.
- Prayer has been taken from our schools, replaced by the training of our young people in philosophies that are anti-God and anti-Bible.[6]

In an article entitled "America, Return to God," Shirley Dobson quotes from Gary Bauer's book *Our Hopes Our Dreams*:

At least 10 million citizens will be victims of violent crime this year, and 32 million will be victims of property crime.... There is one violent crime every 16 seconds; one murder every 21 minutes; one forcible rape every five minutes; one robbery every 48 seconds; one aggravated assault every 28 seconds; and one property crime every three seconds.[7]

But what we see as the world's pain and disillusionment, God has always seen as opportunity. As the poignant words of the song state:

Empty people filled with care,
  headed who knows where.
On the go through private pain,
  living fear to fear.
Laughter hides their silent cry,
  that only Jesus hears.[8]

They are as the psalmist who said, "My soul thirsts for Thee, my flesh yearns for Thee, in a dry and weary land where there is no water" (Ps. 63:1). Isaiah states:

> Encourage the exhausted, and strengthen the feeble. Say to those with anxious heart, "Take courage, fear not. Behold, your God will come with vengeance; the recompense of God will come, but He will save you." Then the eyes of the blind will be opened, and the ears of the deaf will be unstopped. Then the lame will leap like a deer, and the tongue of the dumb will shout for joy. For waters will break forth in the wilderness and streams in the Arabah. And the scorched land will become a pool, and the thirsty ground springs of water (Isa. 35:3-7).

Come sweet River!

57

The River Flows from His Temple, and We Are His Temple

At this very feast hundreds of years earlier, Solomon's Temple was dedicated, and the priests could not stand to minister because the Temple was filled with the glory of the Lord (see 1 Kings 8:2,11).

It was also on "the great day" of the Feast of Tabernacles that Haggai prophesied of a greater glory coming to the Temple (see Hag. 2:1). "'I will fill this house with glory,' says the Lord of hosts. 'The latter glory of this house will be greater than the former'" (Hag. 2:7,9).

It is no coincidence these two events transpired during the same feast. Because of the Holy Spirit's orchestration of the timing of their occurrence and Christ's later declaration at this precise moment, we are able to understand that these events all picture the same thing—the river of God's Spirit coming to take up His abode in us as we drink of the fountain of life. We are now the temple of the Holy Spirit (see 1 Cor. 3:16; 6:19), filled with His glory. And the glory in us is far greater than that in the former Temple.

If this were all the revelation contained in this passage, it would be wonderful, but the reservoir runs deeper still. Jesus said, "He who believes in me...from his *innermost being* shall flow rivers of living water" (John 7:38, italics mine). "Innermost being" is translated from the word *koilia*, which literally means "womb." It is actually translated as such in Matthew 19:12, Luke 1:15 and numerous other references. Of course, a womb speaks of reproduction, of birthing or bringing forth life.

Rivers of Living Water

The phrase "rivers of living water" is used again in Revelation 22:1,2, where it is translated "river of the water of life." The passage in Revelation describes Jesus as the source of life. Out of Him flows a river with trees on either side. Leaves are produced by the trees that are fed by the river that is fed by Jesus. People—the nations—partake of the life of the leaves and are made whole.

We must understand there is no difference between the river of life one day flowing out of the Lamb, bringing healing and wholeness to the whole earth, and the rivers of living water that should now be flowing from the Church. Christ was saying:

- The life in Me will one day flow from you.
- The river in Me will flow from your womb.
- That which I am birthing, you will carry for Me and release into the earth.
- The harvest I am producing will be birthed from the womb of the Church.

The river Ezekiel saw originated from *the Temple*: "Then he brought me back to the door of the house; and behold, water was flowing from under the threshold of the house toward the east, for the house faced east" (Ezek. 47:1). This house was the temple, and that temple is us. We are now the temple of the Holy Spirit.

The river of life that Ezekiel saw and Jesus spoke of is now flowing from us, the Church. We are His birthing vessels, His incubation chambers releasing life to those around us. Why should this surprise us? Is it not supposed to be the very life of Jesus in us that we are ministering to the earth?

Yes, We Deliver!
John 7:39 tells us, "But this He spoke of the Spirit." It is the Spirit of God flowing from us. He doesn't lay hands on the sick. We lay hands on the sick. He doesn't lay hands on a person and ordain—He tells us to do it for Him. The Holy Spirit, inside of us, releases a river to flow into that person, and they are now anointed and appointed by God. When He wants to bring forth the gospel, which is the power of God unto salvation and life, He does not

59

> God doesn't just speak from the clouds.
> He speaks from His people.

echo it from the heavens. He speaks it through us. God's life, the literal power and energy of God, flows out of our mouths and penetrates the hearts of unbelievers, and they are born again.

We are the ones who wield the sword of the Spirit—the spoken Word of God. When the Spirit of God wants to cut and bring judgment into situations, He doesn't just speak from the clouds. He speaks from His people—out of our spirits. When I speak His Word into a situation at the direction of the Holy Spirit, it is as if the Lamb of God Himself spoke the Word. It releases God's life! We are the womb of God from which the river is supposed to flow.

Amazing. We are the "birthers" of the Spirit of God on the earth. Oh, I realize we've often been too anemic in times past to bear children. "Children have come to birth, and there [was] no strength to deliver" (Isa. 37:3).

"The harvest truly is plenteous, but the laborers [have been] few" (Matt. 9:37, *KJV*). But God has had a plan. The river is increasing in its depth.

"'Shall I bring to the point of birth, and not give delivery?' says the Lord" (Isa. 66:9). The answer is no, and even now we are receiving strength to deliver. We will give birth to this harvest, this feast of ingathering.

Preparing for the Harvest

The Son has asked for the nations as His inheritance (see Ps. 2:8), and He is too irresistible for the Father to refuse. The zeal of the Father for His Son will accomplish it (see Isa. 9:7). Henry Ford once said, "Obstacles are those frightful things you see when you take your eyes off your goal."[9] The Father and the Son have never taken their eyes off the goal and neither should we.

But back to our original question. Why is this present renewal—and in some places revival—being referred to as "the river"? By connecting this current outpouring with the river, the Holy Spirit is saying—if it is Him making that connection, and I believe it is—the river of life is about to flow from the Church in *unprecedented* ways; the harvest coming is indeed a *great* harvest. The feast of ingathering is taking place. The plowman *will* overtake the reaper. The former and latter rains are coming simultaneously. The threshing floors will be overwhelmed, the vats will overflow.

If we are wise we will prepare. Better to be ready and it not happen than to be unready and have it catch us unawares. The signs are overwhelming that the harvest is beginning. Let us be wise in our preparations and ready to reap. The ripe harvest must become a reaped harvest.

Cramming Suitcases and Filling God's People
As we consider readiness for the harvest, I want to share a final thought concerning preparation from this passage in John. In order for us to have the river flowing from us, one drink from the

fountain is not enough. We must drink *continuously*.

The two verbs "come" and "drink" are in the present imperative tense. This means it is a command—not just an invitation—
and involves continuous or repeated action. Christ was saying,
"*Keep* coming to me and *keep* drinking!" So often we try to live
on yesterday's manna. Just as the Israelites, however, we must
have "daily bread," and we must take a "daily drink."

This is what is meant by Ephesians 5:18, "be filled with the
Spirit." Once again, the tense is present imperative. He is *com-
manding* us to *continually* be filled with the Spirit.

How do we reconcile this with verses such as John 1:16, "For
of His fulness we have all received"? We *have* received the fullness of Christ, but we must *stay* filled with His Spirit. We can be
100 percent saved but walk in 30 percent power and efficiency.

After speaking on this subject, Dwight Moody was asked why
he needed to be filled and refilled with the Spirit. "That's very
simple," said Mr. Moody, "I leak."

All of us do. That's why we must drink continually in order to
stay filled with the Spirit. While studying the word "filled"
(Greek: *pleroo*), I found the definition "to cram" something full.
This didn't seem like a very scholarly definition, but it sure com-
municated to me.

My wife and kids showed me how to cram something full
when we packed for vacation. I finished one of the suitcases and
said, "This one is full."

My precious Ceci gave me one of those looks that was a combination of sympathy, bewilderment and disgust. "You silly
man," she said. "Who taught you how to pack?"

"Guys don't need to be taught how," I said rather *male-ly*.

"Girls," she called to Sarah and Hannah, "come here. Your
daddy thinks this suitcase is full."

They gave me the same look she had given. (Sometimes I
think women sit around and practice their *looks*. "Okay, girls,
now this is the 'please' look. Good. This is the 'I can't believe
you said that' look. Very good. This is the 'you silly man' look.
Excellent!")

One of them spoke up and said, "Let's show Dad how to *fill* a suitcase."

They proceeded to empty several more drawers and cosmetic cases into the suitcase and then took turns sitting, jumping and standing on it. My girls ran across the room and leaped onto the suitcase.

I stood watching in awe.

Finally, with all three of them standing on it, one of them looked at me and said, "Snap it closed."

I quickly obeyed—you couldn't have paid me to disobey at this point—then looked at them and asked, "Who taught you how to do that?"

"Girls don't need to be taught how," my daughter replied rather *female-ly*. "Now," she said, "the suitcase is full. You may carry it to the car."

62

Did I ever tell you about the back injury I had....

(In order to preserve my family ties, I have been instructed by my wife and children—while giving me an "if you know what's good for you" look—to inform you I have the tendency to exaggerate in some of my stories.)

That suitcase is the picture I have in mind when I think of something being crammed full. The Holy Spirit wants to fill us, push it down, put more in, cram it down, and so on.

He wants us full of Him! Full of the river!

His desire is that we *keep* coming, *keep* drinking and *keep* being filled. Why? So the river can keep flowing. The verb "flow" is also in the present tense. If we *keep* coming and *keep* drinking, we'll *keep* being filled and the river will *keep* flowing.

In our lives we need and want the continual flow. In our homes and marriages we need the continual flow. In our churches we must have the continual flow. Don't let the river dry up in you—a harvest hangs in the balance.

Awaken our thirst, Lord. May we say with the psalmist: "As the deer pants for the water brooks, so my soul pants for Thee, O God. My soul thirsts for God, for the living God" (Ps. 42:1,2).

May we, as King David, have a craving for a drink from the well of Bethlehem (see 2 Samuel 23:15).

If we do, we'll hear You saying, "The Rock has been smitten" (see 1 Cor. 10:4). *You will say to us, "Let the one who is thirsty come; let the one who wishes take the water of life without cost"* (Rev. 22:17).

Notes

1. Jack Canfield and Mark Victor Hansen, *Chicken Soup for the Soul* (Deerfield Beach, FL: Health Communications, Inc., 1993), p. 290. Adapted.
2. Frank Damazio, *Seasons of Revival* (Portland: Bible Temple Publishing, 1996), p. 50.
3. Kevin Conner, *The Feasts of Israel* (Portland: Bible Temple Publications, 1980), p. 88.
4. Edward K. Rowell, *Quotes & Idea Starters for Preaching and Teaching* (Grand Rapids: Baker Books, 1996), p. 142.
5. Craig Brian Larson, *Illustrations for Preaching and Teaching* (Grand Rapids: Baker Books, 1993), p. 264.
6. Damazio, *Seasons of Revival*, adapted from pp. 22, 23.
7. Shirley Dobson, "America, Return to God," *Pray* (March/April 1998).
8. Phill McHugh and Greg Nelson, "People Need the Lord," Shepherd's Fold Music, 1983.
9. Canfield, *Chicken Soup for the Soul*, p. 225.

CHAPTER FOUR

Everything Will Live Where the River Goes

Replete with symbolic pictures, truths and insights, Ezekiel 47:1-12 is, without question, the most complete scriptural passage on the river of God. Like John 7:37-39, this passage links the river of God to the harvest and also makes clear our participation.

The prophet Ezekiel is obviously seeing a vision of the river of life, not a physical river, and the details given are to be understood through spiritual eyes. Let's read it together.

> Then he brought me back to the door of the house; and behold, water was flowing from under the threshold of the house toward the east, for the house faced east. And the water was flowing down from under, from the right side of the house, from south of the altar. And he brought me out by way of the north gate and led me around on the outside to the outer gate by way of the gate that faces east. And behold, water was trickling from the south side.
>
> When the man went out toward the east with a line in his hand, he measured a thousand cubits, and he led me through the water, water reaching the ankles. Again he

measured a thousand and led me through the water, water reaching the knees. Again he measured a thousand and led me through the water, water reaching the loins. Again he measured a thousand; and it was a river that I could not ford, for the water had risen, enough water to swim in, a river that could not be forded. And he said to me, "Son of man, have you seen this?"

Then he brought me back to the bank of the river. Now when I had returned, behold, on the bank of the river there were very many trees on the one side and on the other. Then he said to me, "These waters go out toward the eastern region and go down into the Arabah; then they go toward the sea, being made to flow into the sea, and the waters of the sea become fresh. And it will come about that every living creature which swarms in every place where the river goes, will live. And there will be very many fish, for these waters go there, and the others become fresh; so everything will live where the river goes. And it will come about that fishermen will stand beside it; from Engedi to Eneglaim there will be a place for the spreading of nets. Their fish will be according to their kinds, like the fish of the Great Sea, very many. But its swamps and marshes will not become fresh; they will be left for salt. And by the river on its bank, on one side and on the other, will grow all kinds of trees for food. Their leaves will not wither, and their fruit will not fail. They will bear every month because their water flows from the sanctuary, and their fruit will be for food and their leaves for healing" (Ezek. 47:1-12).

Ezekiel's first point is that the river initiates from the Temple. Verse one refers to it as the "house," but you need only read the preceding verses in chapter 46 to know he is speaking of the Temple. Also, verse 12 calls this house "the sanctuary," confirming it is the Temple. He emphatically states here that the trees on the bank bring life and healing "because their water flows from the sanctuary." This verse also leaves no doubt the river is the same one later mentioned in Revelation 22:1,2:

> And he showed me a river of the water of life, clear as crystal, coming from the throne of God and of the Lamb, in the middle of its street. And on either side of the river was the tree of life, bearing twelve kinds of fruit, yielding its fruit every month; and the leaves of the tree were for the healing of the nations.

Both references say the trees yield fruit every month, and both tell us their leaves are for healing. These are unmistakably the same river. The passage in Revelation is even more specific about the source of the river of life. Not only does it flow from the Temple, it initiates *from the Lamb on the throne, Jesus Christ.*

A great deal more could be written about the source of this river. Thousands of sermons have been preached about Christ being the living water, the well of salvation, the rock Moses struck from which the water gushed, and the river of life issuing from the Lamb. But even though the river flows from Christ, *it also flows from us.* This isn't spoken of nearly as often.

Collaborators with Christ

When the apostle Paul, inspired by the Holy Spirit, said, "Do you not know that you are a temple of God, and that the Spirit of God dwells in you?" (1 Cor. 3:16), he used the Greek word *naos* for "temple," which always referred to the holy of holies. He was literally saying, "Don't you know you are the holy of holies?"

If we are the temple of God and the river flows from the temple, it is then consistent to say the river should flow from us, just as Jesus said. We are God's plan. We're His releasers. We're not the source, but the Source is in us, and He allows us the privilege of being His co-laborers.

The following story is told about a performance of Poland's famous concert pianist and prime minister, Ignace Paderewski.

A young boy was taken to this performance by his mother who wanted to encourage her son's piano playing. They found their seats close to the stage, and while the mother was preoccupied the boy wandered away.

When it was time for the concert to begin, the spotlight came on and a hush settled over the concert hall. Only then was the boy at the majestic Steinway noticed, as he sat innocently picking out "Twinkle, Twinkle, Little Star."

Before the astonished mother could retrieve her son, Paderewski came on stage and quickly moved to the keyboard.

"Don't quit—keep playing," he whispered. The master reached down and began playing a bass part. Then, encircling the child, he reached his other arm around to add a running *obbligato*. Together, the old master and the young novice held the crowd mesmerized.

Our efforts to release the water of life can seem feeble and terribly deficient, but the Master surrounds us and whispers in our ear, time and again, "Don't quit—keep playing." And as we do, He augments and supplements until a work of amazing beauty is created.[1]

It's great to collaborate with the Maestro isn't it?! He sure makes us look good.

Jesus described this source of life-giving in us another way in chapter 4 of the Gospel of John. Though only one English word is used, He actually talked about two types of wells. The well of Jacob (see John 4:11) was a *phrear*, a cistern, or a pit dug to hold water.[2] On the other hand, the well that Christ places in us (see John 4:14) is a *pege*, a fountain which either springs up or flows.[3] We are not simply a storage tank, or cistern, for the living water, but the very *source* of life is in us "*springing up* to eternal life." Cisterns stagnate and dry up; springs remain fresh with a continuous flow.

What a powerful truth! We need not look without us for the source of life. He lives in us.

Going Deeper

Ezekiel 47:3-5 mentions five water levels of increasing depth: at first a trickle, then at the ankles, to the knees, to the loins, till finally there was enough water to swim in, a river that could not be forded. Much has been said and written about these stages of the river. Some say they represent various points in history, with the kingdom of God gaining momentum and influence as we approach the end.

Levels of Maturity

The five river levels could also be related to each of us as individuals, representing different stages of maturity in us. We may have trickles in our lives or mighty flows, depending on our personal walks with the Lord. I don't think the levels of the river in our lives *dictate* our conditions as much as they *reveal* them. In the New Testament we find five Greek words representing five steps of our spiritual growth and development.

- *Nepios* refers to us as *babes* in Christ (see 1 Cor. 3:1).
- *Paidion* speaks of us as children (see 1 John 2:18).
- *Teknon* is also translated as children, but was used for an older child (see John 13:33).
- *Huios* is the word for a fully matured son (see 2 Cor. 6:18).
- *Pater* is the word for father (see 1 John 2:13).

Others believe the levels refer to spiritual truths we must walk in. The knee level, for example, could represent prayer; the loins might represent spiritual reproduction.

My good friend Kenny Price makes the point that the knee level (Hebrew: *berek*) could even represent the *blessing* of the Father. Its root word, *barak*, means both to kneel and to bless.[4] Blessing is the word *berakah* in the Old Testament. There was always a close association between *kneeling* and receiving a *blessing*. Bless, *barak*, is used in Numbers 6:22-27 to describe Aaron's priestly blessing of the Lord's presence, grace and keeping power. Verse 27 states that God's name was to be put on the sons of Israel and God would *bless* them.

Could the knee level be symbolic of our full submission—bowing the knee—to the Lord? And in return His blessing, protection and favor are upon us? Price believes it is and makes a strong case for it.

Levels of Revival

Another supposition is that the different levels represent different stages of any one revival or outpouring of the Holy Spirit. This, of course, could still cover long periods of time, even decades or more. Every movement of the Spirit has a progressive development. Revival is not an instantaneous happening. It is a process. We will talk more about this process in the following chapters.

—

Without character and wisdom sufficient
to sustain us in the river, we can fall into
extremes, presumption or pride.

—

Though an outbreak of revival may seem to spring up overnight, events and circumstances behind the scenes have set the stage.

One interesting observation about these levels is they increased every 1,000 cubits. The study of numbers in Scripture should never be anything we base doctrine on, but it does give us interesting insights into biblical patterns. Without question, there is validity to this. The number 1,000 in Scripture, being a multiple of ten, represents the *perfection or completion of divine order*. This suggests God brings us to completion at each of these levels before taking us to the next level. He expects *order* at each stage.

Many people find it too difficult to stand in the river of God, even where the water comes up only to their ankles. They are knocked off their feet by the blessings or gifts released at this depth. Without character and wisdom sufficient to sustain them, they fall into extremes, presumption, pride or other sins. As Balaam the prophet, whose gift led to monetary temptations, we, too, run the same risk. A few miracles take place, or perhaps a slew of conversions, and we often think of a way to turn it into gain. At each stage God proves us to see if we can steward what He has given before entrusting to us another level.

> Think a moment about a water-saturated sponge. If we push down with our finger even slightly, water runs out onto the table. We immediately know what fills the interior pockets of the sponge.
>   The same is true of ourselves. We can tell what fills us on the inside by what comes out under pressure.[5]

71

That pressure is often a little success. Later in this book we will discuss more thoroughly the potential for abuses and extremes which can accompany a move of the Holy Spirit.

Refreshing, Living Waters

The direction Ezekiel's river began to flow also has great significance. "These waters go out toward the eastern region and go down into the Arabah; then they go toward the sea, being made to flow into the sea, and the waters of the sea become fresh" (Ezek. 47:8).

The Arabah mentioned is the low region into which the valley of the Jordan River runs near Jericho. The Hebrew word *arabah* means "dry land, desert or wilderness."[6] It has the strong sense of sterility. Ezekiel is using this term to describe the lifeless condition of the world. Isaiah 14:17 states that Satan "made the world like a wilderness and overthrew its cities."

The sea mentioned in Ezekiel's vision is the Dead Sea, which also symbolizes the "dead sea" of fallen humankind. Nothing lives in the Dead Sea. The low state to which the human race has fallen is further depicted when we realize the Dead Sea is the lowest elevation point of any land surface on earth, 1294 feet *below* sea level. The symbolism is unmistakable. These living waters are released from the temple of God and through us are to flow into the dead sea of humanity bringing life—"the waters of the sea become fresh."

"Fresh" is *rapha*, which means "to heal." It is the same word used in the phrase from Exodus 15:26, "For I, the Lord, am your healer." Spiritually dead humanity is going to be healed when it comes into contact with the river. The heart of God screams the point in Ezekiel 47:9, "*Everything will live where the river goes!*" (italics and exclamation point mine).

The Fish Are Multiplying!

Twice Ezekiel tells us there will be "very many" fish (verses 9 and 10). This is symbolic of the harvest we see beginning throughout the world today.

- 28,000 people a day are being born again in China.
- 20,000 people a day are being born again in Africa.
- 35,000 people a day are being born again in Latin America.
- Christianity is the fastest-growing movement in the world with a 6.9 percent growth rate, compared to 2.7 percent for Islam, 2.2 percent for Hinduism and 1.7 percent for Buddhism.
- In 1900 there were no known Christians in Korea; now 40 percent of the population is Christian.
- In 1950 China had one million believers. By 1980 there were 40 million and 75 million by 1992.
- In Iran, more people have been converted to Christ in the past 10 years than in the previous 1,000 years.
- Latin Americans are getting saved at a rate four times faster than the population growth. In 1900 there were only 50,000 born-again believers in the Latin countries; by 1980 there were 20 million. By the year 2000 their ranks are expected to grow to more than 100 million.

- In Saudi Arabia during the Persian Gulf war, more than 100 churches were planted.[7]

As encouraging as these statistics are, however, we must remember that much of the world is still a wilderness waiting for the flow of God's river.

Waters Will Break Forth in the Desert

Numerous Scriptures refer to God "life-ing" the wilderness. Isaiah 35 is a tremendous chapter describing God's life and healing flowing to these places of death. Though we mentioned it in chapter 3, it is worth reading again here.

> The *wilderness* and the *desert* will be glad, and the *Arabah* will rejoice and blossom; like the crocus it will blossom profusely and rejoice with rejoicing and shout of joy. The glory of Lebanon will be given to it, the majesty of Carmel and Sharon. They will see the glory of the Lord, the majesty of our God. Encourage the exhausted, and strengthen the feeble. Say to those with anxious heart, "Take courage, fear not. Behold, *your God will come* with vengeance; the recompense of God will come, but *He will save you.*" Then the eyes of the blind will be opened, and the ears of the deaf will be unstopped. Then the lame will leap like a deer, and the tongue of the dumb will shout for joy. *For waters will break forth in the wilderness and streams in the Arabah.* And the scorched land will become a pool, and the thirsty ground springs of water; in the haunt of jackals, its resting place, grass becomes reeds and rushes (Isa. 35:1-7, italics mine).

Isaiah 41:17,18 is another great passage:

The afflicted and needy are seeking water, but there is none, and their tongue is parched with thirst; *I, the Lord, will answer them Myself,* as the God of Israel I will not forsake them. *I will open rivers* on the bare heights, and springs in the midst of the valleys; *I will make the wilderness a pool of water,* and the dry land fountains of water (italics mine).

Can you hear the heart of God in these verses? He is deeply moved with compassion by the thirst and torment of those in the wilderness. "I *will* answer them *Myself,*" He declares. "I will not forsake them." Mr. River Himself is, with great intensity, flowing to the dry places of the earth.

He Paid Full Price

God reminds me of a small boy attracted to a "Puppies For Sale" sign above the door of a store.

The boy entered the store and asked the owner how much the puppies cost. "From $30 to $50," the owner replied.

Reaching into his pocket, the boy pulled out several coins. "I have $2.37," he said. "Can I please see them?"

The proprietor smiled and whistled. Out of a kennel came Lady, followed by five tiny, adorable puppies. One puppy, however, was lagging considerably behind. Immediately, the boy's attention was on the slower, limping puppy. "What's wrong with that one?" he asked.

The owner explained that his veterinarian had discovered the puppy was missing a hip socket. "It will always be lame and walk with a limp," he added.

The little boy became very excited and said, "I'll take that one."

"Naw," the owner argued. "I couldn't sell you that one. He's flawed. If you really want him, I'll just give him to you."

The little boy became angry, looked the owner in the eye, pointed his finger at him and said, "I don't want you to give him to me. This puppy is worth just as much as these other puppies. And I will pay full price. I'll give you

$2.37 now and 50 cents a month until I have paid for him."

"But young man," the owner persisted, "you really don't want this puppy. He won't be able to run and jump and play with you like the others could."

The young boy reached down and rolled up his pant leg, revealing a badly twisted, crippled left leg supported by a metal brace. He looked up at the store owner and softly replied, "Well, I don't run so well myself, and this little puppy will need someone who understands."[8]

Christ came not for the healthy, but for the sick;
not for the righteous, but for sinners.
And He paid full price!

God sent Christ to identify with our weaknesses. He suffered loss, pain, rejection and separation from God. He came not for the healthy, but for the sick; not for the righteous, but for sinners (see Mark 2:17).

And He paid the full price!

Birth Pangs in the Wilderness

"Behold, I will do something new, now it will spring forth; will you not be aware of it? I will even make a roadway in the wilderness, *rivers in the desert*" (Isa. 43:19, italics mine).

Psalm 29:8 states this truth in a different but powerful way, "The voice of the Lord shakes the wilderness." Here "shake" is the Hebrew word *chuwl* which means travail, birth pangs or to give birth. It is the same word as "calve" in verse nine.

Rotherham actually translates the phrase, "The voice of Yahweh bringeth birth pains upon the wilderness."[9]

The New English Bible says, "The voice of the Lord makes the wilderness writhe in travail."[10]

The consistency of river symbolism is so great in Scripture it makes the interpretation of Ezekiel 47 and other passages unques-tionable. The river represents God's life flowing to the lost. These verses are being fulfilled in this hour. God is taking a world that Satan turned into a wilderness—sterile, lifeless, empty—and is causing His river to flow to it. Birth pangs are everywhere!

Signs of the Times

As I stand with Ezekiel of old, looking upon the "dry bones" of the world, I, too, can hear the question from the aching heart of a passionate God, "Can these bones live?" (see Ezek. 37:1-14).

There are approximately 4 billion of these "spiritual skele-tons" scattered throughout the earth. They come disguised as teenagers, yuppies, baby boomers, retirees, Buddhists, Muslims, atheists, humanists, feminists, liberals, conservatives and in just about any other cloak you can imagine. They're hungry and look-ing for the wind...the breath...the river.

We must give them an opportunity to live!

"Opportunity is in respect to time, in some sense, as time is in respect to eternity: it is the small moment, the exact point, the critical minute, on which every good work so much depends."[11]

Webster defines opportunity as "a set of circumstances pro-viding a *chance* or *possibility*; a stroke of good fortune which presents itself and *can either be grasped or lost*"[12] (italics mine). Opportunities come and go. Sometimes they return; often they don't. We've all heard the phrase, "window of opportunity."

The concept of opportune time is found in the Greek word *kairos*. It is the time something *should* or *must* be done. *Chronos* is the Greek word for the *general* time something *is* done. The distinction is important.

In Matthew 16:3 Christ rebuked the Pharisees for their inabili-ties to discern the signs of the times (*kairos*). Later, in Luke 19:44, He prophesied the future destruction of Jerusalem as He wept over it, and He revealed the primary cause for the city's demise: "You did not recognize the time (*kairos*) of your visitation."

On the other hand, Paul commended the Thessalonian church for its ability to discern the times (*chronos*) and seasons (*kairos*) (see 1 Thess. 5:1). Of this church Paul also said, "You became an example to all the believers in Macedonia and in Achaia" (1 Thess. 1:7).

For those Jesus wept over in Jerusalem, the opportunity did not return. Nor did it return for Moses' generation of Israelites. Regardless of the obstacles, we must be prepared to seize opportunities before the window closes. Someone once said that opportunity is a good deal more conspicuous on the way out than on the way in.

Opportunity Knocks When You're in the Shower

A *kairos* opportune time can be somewhat enigmatic—it often comes at a most inopportune time. As far as convenience is concerned, the opportune time is not always an opportune time. It may not be anticipated and often requires a lot of adjustments and quick maneuvering to take advantage of it. Simply stated, *convenience is totally irrelevant where opportunity is concerned!*

For example, there was the phone call I received in 1976. I was single at the time and working a secular job. The conversation went something like this:

"Hello, Dutch, this is Brother ------. You know the missions trip we have planned for Guatemala that is scheduled to leave tomorrow?"

"Yes, I'm well aware of it."

"Well, we're very short of workers, especially those with experience on these types of trips." These were work teams going into Guatemala to build small, one-room dwellings for the victims of the earthquake of 1976. We would build them a home during the day, then preach the gospel to them at night, telling them it was Christ's love motivating us to be there. It was a most effective evangelistic concept, and I had already been on two or three of these trips.

"So, what do you need from me?" I asked.

"We could really use you on this trip," he said.

In shock, I responded, "Let me get this straight. You're leaving with a team *in the morning* for Guatemala, and you want me to go."

"Yes. We desperately need you."

My mind was racing. "It's Sunday," I said. "I have no way to even speak to my employer today to ask for time off. I would have to be at my workplace at 7:00 A.M. when it opens—with my bags packed—to ask him for 10 days off work, starting *right then!*" (My employer was quite the heathen, by the way.)

"And even if he lets me go, I have no money," I continued. "I've spent all my savings on the previous trips." These trips were costing each participant $600 to $750.

"We believe God will supply the money by morning," he replied. "Just pray about it and call me back." I prayed...then packed.

Two or three acquaintances of mine who heard about the call volunteered the needed money late that evening. Early the next morning I headed for my heathen employer, ready to lose my job. Not only did he tell me I could go—and keep my job—but *I could go on as many of these trips as I desired.* Just try and give him a little more notice next time!

That morning I was on the plane to Guatemala.

What a hassle that opportunity was! How inconvenient!

I can't recall now whether that was the trip when the Lord used us in a remote village to deliver a little demonized girl, six or seven years old. She was so wild and uncontrollable she lived in her parents' backyard *chained to a tree like a dog.* (I relate details of this experience in my book, *Intercessory Prayer.*) Or perhaps it was the trip when the little four-year-old girl living in the cardboard shanty with her mother became so attached to me and I to her. I never have gotten that piece of my heart back. Then again, it could have been the trip when the paralyzed lady was instantly healed, resulting in the salvation of several others.

I hope you get the picture. I would have missed one of the greatest experiences of my life had I not seized that inopportune opportunity. God never said the harvest was *convenient*. He said it was *ripe*. Farmers don't harvest when it is convenient; they harvest when the crop is ripe.

Sinners Are in Season

Say yes to your adventure with God. He has created a great *kairos* season of spiritual harvest on earth. Obviously, we live in a day of staggering, unprecedented change. Even as I write, I'm looking at amazing, irrefutable evidence of this—a piece of the Berlin Wall. This small bit of mortar speaks volumes, not the least of which is *change*. A friend of mine chipped it from the Wall at Checkpoint Charlie in May of 1990. I've stood at that infamous barrier and experienced firsthand the mixture of emotion and pain it generated. I can easily remember the fear and oppression I felt while there in 1986. Fittingly, it was a dark, dreary, cold and rainy day.

In December 1991, however, I drove freely from what used to be West Germany into former East Germany, unimpeded, unquestioned...and *unshot*! Without fear, we drove up to one of the empty guard towers for a closer look. I could envision the machine-gun-toting guards as they used to patrol this border. It was incredibly moving.

But that's old news! The Berlin Wall was several events ago. Since then we've fought a major war in the Middle East. We're now talking about the *former* Soviet Union. The face of Europe is almost unrecognizable, as the vicelike grip of communism has lost its evil hold. From November 1991 to April 1992, 18 new nations were established. What used to be events that would characterize a century—or at least a generation—have now begun happening with astonishing regularity. Other changes, of lesser note yet certainly momentous, seem to happen almost routinely.

This is only the geopolitical scene, however. Add to it changes in the social, cultural, economic, technological and spiritual realms among others. It is safe to say there has never been a generation that has even come remotely close to living through the kinds of changes we're experiencing. George Otis, Jr., in his book *The Last of the Giants*, quotes from Vartan Gregorian, president of Brown University, who states, "Potential knowledge, meaning available information, is now doubling every five years."[13] That means textbooks now being written will be obsolete in a matter of months!

The God who "changes the times and the seasons" (Dan. 2:21, *NKJV*) has sure been busy lately! The God who changes not is sure changing everything else! And if we, the Body of Christ, are to successfully face the issues of our day, we must have enough foresight to be prepared for the opportunities these changes create.

Far too often we, the Church, find ourselves irrelevant, answering questions no one is asking and dealing with issues that no longer exist. Sinners really don't care much about eschatology or whether we baptize by immersion or sprinkling. If we are to seize the opportunities, we must be a relevant and opportunistic people, ready "in season (*eukairos*) and out of season (*akairos*)" (2 Tim. 4:2).

You Can't Build a Fire with Rotten Wood

One of the essential elements that builds readiness is vision. True vision produces both alertness and availability. When you and I have no vision, He has no vessel. "Visionlessness" creates indifference, which must be categorized with the lukewarm status of Revelation 3:16. If I understand this and other Scriptures properly, I think God prefers coldness to indifference and apathy.

Anti-vision can be dealt with because it is so easily recognizable. The "cold" of Revelation 3:16 and sinners who oppose the work of God are not the problems. Passive, apathetic, visionless *believers* are God's problem. We, the Body of Christ, are the folks He has to work through.

"Where there is no vision, the people perish" (Prov. 29:18, KJV). One of the derivatives of the word "perish" is "perishable." Mr. Webster tells me it means, "liable to decay or deterioration."[14] So I looked up decay: "To lose gradually its original form, quality or value."[15] It also mentioned rotten wood and a bad tooth as examples of decay.

I remember stepping onto a rotten log once to cross a stream. It didn't work out too well; rotten wood won't support a whole lot. In fact, it's not good for much of anything. You can't build with it. It's no good for a fire. Sort of reminds me of people who have no vision: They won't support anything. You can't build with them, and you're certainly not going to get any fire out of them. Ever share a dream with visionless people? I'd rather step on a rotten log.

> Lack of vision is like an abscessed tooth! It will infect the Body, eating away productivity and robbing us of our value.

Then there's the tooth picture—the bad tooth as an example of the word "decay." I thought immediately of Proverbs 25:19. It compares confidence in an unfaithful man to a bad tooth. I can't think of anything worse than being compared to a toothache. Ever had one? Most of us have. I once knew a person with an abscessed tooth—ate a hole right through his sinus cavity. It made his entire body sick for a couple of weeks.

That's what lack of vision will do. It all fits. Proverbs 29:18 tells us that *perish* is what happens to those without vision. *Decay* is one of the definitions of perish, pictured by a *bad tooth*. In case you didn't connect all that, let me state it plainly: Lack of vision is like an abscessed tooth! It will infect the whole Body. It eats away productivity and robs us of our value.

Open the Floodgates!

Sometimes we are mesmerized into indifference by the rapid changes taking place around us. It's a small world after all. We hear and see the major events and problems of the entire planet on the screen every evening after dinner. As a result, callousness gradually hardens our minds and emotions to the challenges and needs of the world. Remember, to decay means, "to lose *gradually* its original form, quality and value." It often is a very gradual and subtle thing, similar to the loss of our first love. We're desensitized into indifference. The flow stops, and stagnation sets in.

We need a wake-up call! It's time to rise and shine (see Isa. 60:1). The world is a mess. The "deep darkness" is here, and it's time for His glory to rise upon us who are the light of the world and the city on the hill (see Isa. 60:2; Matt. 5:14). People in darkness always look for light. Tag, we're it.

This shining, however, will only materialize if we care—*really care*—passionately...intensely! We upon whom the ends of the ages have come, what manner of persons ought we to be? (see 1 Cor. 10:11 and 2 Pet. 3:11).

Releasers of the river of God!

The source of the life of God on the earth is through the Body of Christ.

- If it flows to the nations, it will be through the Church.
- If it flows to our nation, it will be from the Church.
- If it flows to our neighbors, our city, it will flow from us, the temple.

Scary, isn't it? Imagine how God must feel sometimes.

If the river is to flow from us to the world around us in the way the Lord wants it to, we must awaken to our destiny. It was said of King David that he "served the purpose of God in his own generation" (Acts 13:36). Will we?

Now is the time for vision! The state of affairs cries out for some passion. Passion means "intense or violent emotion." The dictionary actually said it was used as a word for "the martyrdom of an early Christian."[16] That'll work! That's what I'm speaking of—the kind of intense desire and commitment one will die for. Dr. Eleanor Chestnut had this kind of passion:

In *From Jerusalem to Irian Jaya*, Ruth Tucker writes about Dr. Eleanor Chestnut. After arriving in China in 1893 under the American Presbyterian missions board, Dr. Chestnut built a hospital, using her own money to buy bricks and mortar. The need for her services was so great, she performed surgery in her bathroom until the building was completed.

One operation involved the amputation of a common laborer's leg. Complications arose and skin grafts were needed. A few days later, another doctor asked Chestnut why she was limping. "Oh, it's nothing," was her terse reply.

Finally, a nurse revealed that the skin graft for the patient, a coolie, came from Dr. Chestnut's own leg, taken with only local anesthetic.

During the Boxer Rebellion of 1905, Dr. Chestnut and four other missionaries were killed by a mob that stormed the hospital.[17]

Research tells a statistical horror story of what is happening *every day* in America with our children:

- 1,000 unwed teenage girls become mothers
- 1,106 teenage girls get abortions
- 4,219 teenagers contract sexually transmitted diseases
- 500 adolescents begin using drugs
- 1,000 adolescents begin drinking alcohol
- 135,000 kids bring guns or other weapons to school
- 3,610 teens are assaulted; 80 are raped
- 2,200 teens drop out of high school
- 6 teens commit suicide.[18]

Where are the tears?

Where is the passionate outcry for the lost?

Where is the needed sense of urgency?

These missing pieces of the harvest puzzle will be found at the feet of Jesus, the most passionate and greatest martyr of all. Let Him flow through you.

Louis Pasteur, the pioneer of immunology, lived at a time when thousands of people died each year of rabies. Pasteur had worked for years on a vaccine. Just as he was about to begin experimenting on himself, a nine-year-old, Joseph Meister, was bitten by a rabid dog. The boy's mother begged Pasteur to experiment on her son. Pasteur injected Joseph for ten days—and the boy lived.

Decades later, of all the things Pasteur could have had etched on his headstone, he asked for three words: JOSEPH MEISTER LIVED.

Our greatest legacy will be those who live eternally because of our efforts.[19]

May our epitaphs read, THE DRY BONES LIVED.

Notes

1. Craig Brian Larson, *Illustrations for Preaching and Teaching* (Grand Rapids: Baker Books, 1993), p. 221. Adapted.
2. James Strong, *The New Strong's Exhaustive Concordance of the Bible* (Nashville: Thomas Nelson Publishers, 1990), ref. no. 5421.
3. Spiros Zodhiates, *Hebrew-Greek Key Study Bible—New American Standard* (Chattanooga: AMG Publishers, 1984; revised edition, 1990), p. 1867.
4. Ibid., p. 1716.
5. Larson, *Illustrations for Preaching and Teaching*, p. 22.
6. Zodhiates, *Hebrew-Greek Key Study Bible—New American Standard*, p. 1762.

7. Frank Damazio, *Seasons of Revival* (Portland: Bible Temple Publishing, 1996), pp. 51,52. Adapted.

8. Jack Canfield and Mark Victor Hansen, *Chicken Soup for the Soul* (Deerfield Beach, FL: Health Communications, Inc., 1993), pp. 65, 66. Adapted.

9. *Twenty-Six Translations of the Bible* (Atlanta: Mathis Publishers, 1985), p. 1779.

10. Ibid., p. 1779.

11. Elon Foster, *6000 Classic Sermon Illustrations* (Grand Rapids: Baker Books, reprinted 1993) p. 603.

12. *New Webster's Dictionary and Thesaurus of the English Language* (New York: Lexicon Publications, Inc., 1991 edition), p. 704.

13. George Otis, Jr., *The Last of the Giants* (Tarrytown, NY: Fleming H. Revell Company, 1991), p. 32.

14. *New Webster's Dictionary and Thesaurus of the English Language*, p. 747.

15. Ibid., p. 248.

16. Ibid., p. 734.

17. Edward K. Rowell, *Fresh Illustrations for Preaching and Teaching* (Grand Rapids: Baker Books, 1997), p. 176.

18 . Josh McDowell and Bob Hostetler, *Right from Wrong* (Dallas: Word Publishing, 1994), p. 6.

19. Rowell, *Fresh Illustrations for Preaching and Teaching*, p. 50.

CHAPTER FIVE

Heaping or Level?

Having discussed this glorious river of God—and how it is going to flow in and through us and will result in a great harvest—now it's time to talk about a few unpleasant words. Repentance, cleansing, shaking, discipline, purging and process—these concepts are all involved in the release of the river.

By putting these words on paper, I have already violated several American church rules of success, growth and high sales. Just the mention of these hard sayings transgresses "seeker-sensitive," "user-friendly," "don't be controversial or radical" and "make people feel good" principles.

PLEASE DON'T PUT THE BOOK DOWN! I don't like words like "purging" and "process" myself. They offend me, just as they do you.

I don't like the concept of living at the Cross daily. A Cross-less Christianity is much more appealing.

I hate self-denial.

I detest discipline.

I like gain without pain.

I like prosperity without paying the price.

I like harvest without farming.

I much prefer our modern "what's in it for me?" gospel to the one in the Bible.

I like revival, not the *process* of revival.

Recipe for Revival

I don't like the word "process." I'm a cart-before-the-horse kind of guy, always wanting to skip the cause and get to the effect. I cry, "Show me your works!" God responds by teaching me His *ways*. Process usually implies things such as work and waiting, which I'm against—as are most Americans, including American Christians. We don't realize how much we have been conformed to the world (see Rom. 12:1,2).

We shop for churches the way the world shops, looking for the best deal and flashiest product. We build churches the way the world builds, with an eye toward innovation and outward appearances. And we sell our gospel the way the world sells, with technique and packaging and by appealing to selfish desires. More on this later—if you make it that far.

Process? Journey? Build? Very un-American, un-Christian and un-Dutch. I'm into instant and easy. I don't want to *develop* fruit, I want to *have* fruit. Luscious, heavy, juicy, automatic fruit. I don't want to *sow*, I want to *reap*. I don't want to *build* a church, I want mine to *explode* so I can be the "biggest," "fastest" and "on the leading, cutting edge." How else can I get my name in Christian magazines and on Christian television?

After all, this is America. And we Americans are into enterprise, overnight success and competition. We're capitalists, after all. We like instant gratification, not *process*.

Is It True There Are No Dumb Questions?

My personal propensity toward instant and easy can perhaps best be seen in my cooking. I'm into can openers and microwaves. That's about as deep into the *process* of cooking I get. I recall one evening needing to satisfy my sweet tooth.

"Ceci," I called, "do we have any brownies?"

"No," she replied, "but we have some brownie mix."

"Good. Can you make some?"

"The girls and I are really enjoying this program," she

answered. "Besides, we think it's about time you learn to make brownies. It's really simple."

Me, bake? I thought. *What did I do to deserve this kind of treatment? I don't bake brownies, I eat them. Besides, they're just watching some silly girl show; I'm watching a football game. Women are supposed to bond in the kitchen doing things like this.*

I told them as much.

Some things are better left unsaid. Six eyes bore into me like Clint Eastwood staring down bad guys. "Just kidding," I said as I thought, *Why do women have to be so sensitive?*

"What's the matter?" my sweet daughter Hannah asked. "Are you afraid you can't do it?"

"Yeah," Sarah echoed.

"Now, girls," Mom interjected, "you know he would never admit that. He's a man, and men won't admit they can't do something. And they certainly would never admit to fear."

"Hey," I said, "why do you have to make this a male-female thing?"

Off to the kitchen I went. It really wasn't all that complicated, and Ceci was gracious enough to answer a few questions I asked just to make her feel good. Everything was going well until I came to the "one tablespoon of water."

I stuck my head into the living room and asked, "Only one tablespoon of water?"

"Yeah."

"Level or heaping?" I asked.

Was there any mercy in this woman? Not at that moment. She gave me one of those practiced looks I spoke of earlier. This was sort of an "I'm desperately trying not to burst into uncontrollable laughter, but you sure are making it hard" look. I wondered why she was shaking—just cold, I guess.

"Heaping," she mumbled through the shakes.

It really didn't dawn on me until I tried to heap the water.

Sticking my head back into the living room I said, "Pretty funny, huh? I knew that would make you laugh. You probably thought I was serious."

"Naw," she said. "Whatever gave you that idea?" Then looking at the girls she asked, "Do you think it's cold in here?"

Whew! I thought. *Got away with another one!*

Picture Imperfect

I sometimes ask God dumb questions about His *processes,* too.

"Why is this taking so long?"

"Do I really need this?"

"Where is the shortcut?"

"Can we negotiate?"

"Heaping or level?"

Revival is a *process.* God is into seasoned, well-baked and tender. He is not into instant or microwaveable. And the *process* of revival begins with the *process* of repentance. This repentance is not only personal, but corporate.

The corporate cleansing is often necessary to adjust some of the problems created by a prior season of revival. No revival or

—

> It is difficult, if not impossible, for
> imperfect, unbalanced people to
> manifest the perfect balance of God.

⁓

restoration period is flawless or perfectly balanced. Since God is working through imperfect people, there will always be imperfect movements and organizations. None of us have it totally together. We are all moving from glory to glory (see 2 Cor. 3:18), strength to strength (see Ps. 84:7), faith to faith (see Rom. 1:17) and to brighter and brighter paths (see Prov. 4:18).

Even those ministries and individuals who feel called to fix the rest of us need fixing in places. Imagine that. Much contending for the faith is nothing more than arrogant contentiousness. It reminds me of the brother who died and was receiving a tour of heaven. At one point, Saint Peter took him to a walled-off portion of this great place and motioned for him to be quiet.

"What's the matter?" questioned the man.

"That's ------ on the other side of the wall," answered Peter, naming a certain sect of the church. "They think they're the only ones here."

I think I may know some of those folks, how about you?

Truth isn't usually restored in a totally pure form. Restoration and revival typically don't end up completely balanced. Not because God is deficient, obviously, but because He is working with imperfect people.

- When God emphasizes grace, we often turn it into license.
- When God emphasizes holiness, some make it legalism.
- When God emphasizes power, it is often transformed into sensationalism.
- When God shows up in a particular way, it's very challenging for us not to build a tabernacle and stay there.

It is difficult, if not impossible, for imperfect, unbalanced people to manifest the perfect balance of God. When the waves and tide of an ocean roll in, not only are they comforting and tranquil, but the same water washes ashore lots of debris. Beaches must be continually cleaned, or they can become cluttered and filled with trash.

The same is true with waves of revival. Along with the good they bring, our weaknesses and flesh are also exposed. God, therefore, usually has to put the Church through a seasonal process of cleansing and adjustment between these major outpourings of the Spirit.

Measurable Blockage

Between waves of revival—when the fire wanes—complacency, sin and compromise often set in. This, too, requires a season of adjustment before God can bring a fresh move of His Spirit. If He doesn't purge us with a time of cleansing, the flow of His river in and through us is blocked.

An estimated 500,000 tons of water rush over Niagara Falls every minute. On March 29, 1948, the falls suddenly stopped. People living within the sound of the falls were awakened by the overwhelming silence. They believed it was a sign that the world was coming to an end. It was 30 hours before the rush of water resumed.

What happened? Heavy winds had set the ice fields of Lake Erie in motion. Tons of ice jammed the Niagara River entrance near Buffalo and stopped the flow of the river until the ice shifted again.[1]

The flow of the river of God in our lives can be blocked by sin and complacency. So in His grace, He brings His melting, refining fire.

Many Christians do not understand this process, these in-between times. I have found the Body of Christ knows little about the seasons of the Spirit, because there is such a limited knowledge of His ways. Rather than flow with what God is saying and doing at the time, we superimpose *what we desire Him to be doing and saying*, then convince ourselves of its accuracy through non-biblical, lowered standards of judgment.

In *A View from the Zoo*, Gary Richmond, a former zookeeper, has this to say:

Raccoons go through a glandular change at about 24 months. After that they often attack their owners. Since a 30-pound raccoon can be equal to a 100-pound dog in a scrap, I felt compelled to mention the change coming to a pet raccoon owned by a young friend of mine, Julie. She listened politely as I explained the coming danger.

I'll never forget her answer, "It will be different for me...." And she smiled as she added, "Bandit wouldn't hurt me. He just wouldn't."

Three months later Julie underwent plastic surgery for

facial lacerations sustained when her adult raccoon attacked her for no apparent reason. Bandit was released into the wild.[2]

This young lady judged Bandit based on *what she wanted him to be like*. We often do this with God and His ways. The results are predictable.

For example, we will do much more sowing than reaping during some seasons. Because this offends our concepts of self-worth, success and fruitfulness, we find this hard to accept. So we, in our own strength and wisdom, try to reap in the sowing season. We are driven to success that is *measurable*, which seeds planted underground are not.

What does this have to do with revival or the river? We in the Church have not understood the *process* of revival that involves various *phases* or *seasons*. Thus, we will do almost anything to skip the process and get to the measurable fruit—numbers, miracles, new buildings—anything we can see with our eyes and call success. We then label it as revival or a move of God.

Once this has happened, the standards are lowered and we end up with something less than true revival. Our methods of measuring, in violation of the Scriptures (see 2 Cor. 4:18), are now natural, as are our methods of production. True rivers of revival will never flow until we cast off human methods, rise above human abilities and allow the Spirit of God to plan the strategies and define the results.

False Revivals

Our propensity for lowering the standards for revival and true spirituality has been decried by Watchman Nee. "By the time the average Christian gets his temperature up to normal," he has said, "everybody thinks he's got a fever."

Leonard Ravenhill agrees. "The Church has been subnormal for so long," he says, "that when it finally becomes normal, everybody thinks it's abnormal."[3]

The Early Church, too, turned the world right side up and some called it upside down (see Acts 17:6, *KJV*).

But when we lower our standards of judgment, we move dangerously close to denial. I fear we are like the "never-say-die general who was taken captive and thrown into a deep, wide pit along

———

We can be like thirsty desert travelers.
Often what we think is God's river of revival
is nothing more than a mirage.

———

with a number of his soldiers. In that pit was a huge pile of horse manure. 'Follow me,' the general cried to his men as he dove into the pile, 'There has to be a horse in here somewhere!'"[4]

Optimism can be great, but optimism must be tempered by realism. We have a tendency to label certain movements and events as revival when, in fact, they are not. We can be like thirsty desert travelers, so desirous of water that we see what is not there. Often what we think is God's river of revival is nothing more than a mirage.

Let's look at seven false types and methods of revival that can be found in the Scriptures and in the Church. Identifying and explaining them will help us avoid them.

Rapid Revival

Of course, this is not referring to the sudden thing God sometimes does, but to our quick-fix mindsets determined to have it all *now*. As the seed in the parable of the sower (see Matt. 13:20,21), this type of revival springs up quickly, usually through man-made methods. But lacking firm roots—a foundation laid by the Holy Spirit—it also quickly dies.

Premature Revival

Closely linked to rapid revival, premature revival means to assume revival has arrived before it really has. The movement may truly be of the Holy Spirit, but is only in the infancy stage. Our presumption often causes a premature relaxing of effort or change of strategy and then, of course, momentum is lost.

An example of this can be found in Israel in Haggai's day. Israel began the work of restoring the Temple and, when the foundation was laid, they threw a great party (see Ezra 3:10-13). The work then stopped, however, for 16 years until God raised up Haggai the prophet to confront them concerning the unfinished work of restoration (see Hag. 1,2). The people responded properly and, with God's help, finished the work...16 years after the initial celebration.

"New Cart" Revival

This effort to produce revival is based on man-made methods. When David wanted to bring back to Israel the Ark of the Covenant, which represented the presence and glory of God in their midst, he thought he had a better way than God's prescribed method. Rather than the priests using poles to carry the Ark on their shoulders, David had a nice, new cart made to transport the Ark (see 2 Sam. 6). God responded saying, in essence, "I don't need your new ideas and methods to bring restoration, David. I need obedience." David's presumptuous disobedience cost him the life of one of his men and caused a lengthy delay in restoring the Ark to Jerusalem. We still create many new carts today: man-made methods, plans and programs with which we endeavor to bring revival. The results are costly!

Kitchen Revival

Performance motivation produces this mindset. As Martha in Luke 10:38-42, we cannot bring ourselves to believe sitting at His feet is a higher priority than working. We are forever conjuring up new recipes for revival, scrambling around in our well-equipped kitchens, trying to "cook-up" revival. God, however, is in the living room. Revival is NOT produced, it is born! Born of the Spirit, conceived in relationship. This false method of revival emphasizes works over worship. Jesus said essentially that what it produces will not last.

Sensational Revival

This, of course, is "revival" based on hype, sensation, big-name personalities and, yes, even true miracles. Emotional stirrings are fine and can be used in a positive way. Well-known individuals can—though do not necessarily—give a sense of credibility and be used to attract people. And, of course, miracles are wonderful blessings and can be genuine signs. The risk, however, is that all of these can also be used to manipulate because they appeal to and impress the mind, emotions and flesh, but not necessarily the spirit.

Sensational people or events do get attention, but don't necessarily produce life. When used as the primary blocks for building, they will always lead to extremes, imbalance and the glorifying of people. Biblical examples would be Samson and many of the people who observed Christ's miracles. Even Moses, when he performed a miracle by striking the rock a second time, was severely chastised for doing it with impure motives (see Num. 20:8-13). We must guard against seeking the sensation over the substance!

Stale Revival

Many of us have heard of "the glory days." But some "old-time religion" is nothing more than rut religion. We are very prone to resting on yesterday's experiences and successes. We need daily doses of the bread of Heaven, however, and must *stay* filled with the Spirit (see Eph. 5:18). Ecclesiastes 10:10 tells us, "If the axe is

Though Jesus Christ is the same
yesterday, today and forever,
His methods and movements are not.

dull and he does not sharpen its edge, then he must exert more strength." Though Jesus Christ is the same yesterday, today and forever (see Heb. 13:8), His methods and movements are not. He is never static, nor can we be. Jesus said of the church at Sardis, "You have a name that you are alive, but you are dead" (Rev. 3:1).

Their reputation was still good, but God knew they were really trusting yesterday's experiences and blessings. How easily our wineskins become old and our wine becomes stale. We must guard against this.

Short-Lived Revival
This is a movement of the Holy Spirit that begins well but does not endure. A good beginning does not guarantee a good ending. Many true moves of the Holy Spirit did not end well. The charismatic movement may very well be one of them. It is my opinion that much of what God wanted to accomplish through it was aborted. I will share in more detail of why this happened in a later chapter.

We must allow God to set the standard for the Church, our callings and all our endeavors. Humanity has been trying to lower the criterion since the Fall. We must also come to a greater understanding of the processes involved in attaining that standard.

97

True Revival

Though there is no succinct definition of revival in Scripture, there are examples which give us general principles from which to draw conclusions. From these, as well as modern examples, it is possible to generally define what revival consists of. Here are three different characteristics to look for, according to three different sources.

Renewal of the Church, Conversion of Sinners
Charles Finney said revival "presupposes that the Church is sunk down in a backslidden state....A revival consists in the return of the Church from her backslidings, and in the conversion of sinners." Finney then lists several characteristics of revival:

- A revival always includes conviction of sin on the part of the Church.
- Backslidden Christians will be brought to repentance.

- Christians will have their faith renewed.
- A revival breaks the power of the world and of sin over Christians.
- When the churches are thus awakened and reformed, the reformation and salvation of sinners will follow.[5]

Church Growth and Social Reform

In the book *Rivers of Revival*, Neil Anderson and Elmer Towns discuss the effects of many historical revivals and offer the following summary:

> Each of these revivals was broad in scope, reaching beyond a single religious denomination or ethnic culture. Each of these revivals also appears to have had a significant effect on the society in which they occurred. This influence is reflected in the conversion of large numbers of people, resulting in measurable church growth and significant social reform effected by individuals and/or groups directly related to the revival movement.[6]

The Presence of God and Social Upheaval

In his book, *From Holy Laughter to Holy Fire*, Michael Brown also contends that social reform must be among the fruits of true revival. Brown further suggests that revival in America, when it comes, will be easy to spot.

> What is revival? It is God "stepping down from heaven" and baring His holy arm. He comes and acts and speaks. There is a holy Presence and a word on fire. God is in the midst of His people. The Lord is shaking the world. That is revival! It is a time of visitation. If it is confined to one church, it is not revival. If it is confined to the meetings themselves, it is not revival. If it can all be traced to the efforts of man, it is not revival. If it does not ultimately affect the society, it is not revival.[7]

Describing revival's effect on American culture, Brown contends:

> As long as homosexuals march brazenly down our streets and serve in leading positions in our governments; as long as abortion clinics and pornography theaters thrive; as long as "Christian" young people watch MTV and "Christian" adults watch HBO; as long as the jails have too many prisoners and the mission fields have too few laborers; as long as greed and materialism rule most of the world and much of the church; as long as humanists, new agers and atheists dominate our college faculties; as long as these things are at the forefront of our society, we are not experiencing revival! Sweeping revival in America would mean upheaval. The holy Presence would change the complexion of our nation dramatically.[8]

99

From these biblically based definitions, it is clear America is not yet experiencing true revival. The flow of the river is not very deep. But we can experience it, if we are honest with ourselves and obedient to the Holy Spirit.

According to Reuters news agency, on April 28 at the 1992 Galveston County Fair and Rodeo, a steer named Husker, weighing in at 1,190 pounds, was named grand champion. The steer was sold at auction for $13,500 and slaughtered a few days after the competition. When veterinarians examined the carcass, said a contest official, they found something suspicious. They discovered evidence of what is called "airing."

To give steers a better appearance, competitors have been known to inject air into their animals' hides with a syringe or a needle attached to a bicycle pump. Pump long enough, and they've got themselves what looks like a grand champion steer, though of course it's against the rules.

The Galveston County Fair and Rodeo Association withdrew the championship title and sale money from Husker.[9]

A pumped-up steer illustrates false revival. It may look good temporarily and cause us to feel good for a time, but the results soon disappear.

The Church has perfected the art of "airing" revivals. We must insist on the genuine, a strong flow of the river of God that floods communities and nations with life. It can happen—if we do it God's way.

I'd like it heaping. How about you?

Notes

1. Edward K. Rowell, *Fresh Illustrations for Preaching and Teaching* (Grand Rapids: Baker Books, 1997), p. 126.
2. Craig Brian Larson, *Illustrations for Preaching and Teaching* (Grand Rapids: Baker Books, 1993), p. 231.
3. Michael L. Brown, *From Holy Laughter to Holy Fire* (Shippensburg, PA: Destiny Image Publishers, Inc., 1996), p. 264.
4. Craig Brian Larson, *Contemporary Illustrations for Preachers, Teachers and Writers* (Grand Rapids: Baker Books, 1996), p. 110.
5. Charles G. Finney, *Revival Lectures* (Old Tappan, NJ: Fleming H. Revell Company), pp. 7, 8.
6. Elmer L. Towns and Neil T. Anderson, *Rivers of Revival* (Ventura: Regal Books, 1997), p. 302.
7. Brown, *From Holy Laughter to Holy Fire*, p. 235.
8. Ibid., p. 241.
9. Larson, *Contemporary Illustrations for Preachers, Teachers and Writers*, p. 114.

CHAPTER SIX

I Wish I Knew
What I Was Looking For

It's difficult to find something when you don't know what you're looking for. I recall the night I sat up late trying to turn off the computer. Never did get it turned off.

I had been playing solitaire. That's all I can do on one of those user-friendly beasts—if someone else turns it on for me, that is. I played till about 11:00 P.M., gave up trying to turn it off about 1:00 A.M., and went to bed.

I had tried everything I could think of, clicked YES to every question except, "Do you want to blow up this computer?" I actually said YES to that, too, but backed down when it asked, "Are you sure?"

I thought for a while God might be doing this to me. He's the only one I know who truly has power over computers, and I've heard He even uses surge protectors. But when the temptation to lose my sanctification became more than I could bear, I knew it wasn't Him. The Bible says He won't do that.

Seated at the breakfast table the next morning with red eyes and bags beneath them, Ceci looked at me and asked, "Did you sleep okay?"

"Sure, why?" I replied.

"Because your eyes look like road maps."

"I was up kinda late," I said, hoping she wouldn't pry for the reason.

"Why?" she pried. (Women are curious, you understand. They need to know these sorts of things. A man wouldn't have cared why.)

"Because I couldn't get the computer turned off," I mumbled.

I saw her and our two daughters glance at each other out of the corners of their eyes. They all had goofy "did he say what I think he said?" grins. Finally, one of them could contain herself no longer. "What did you say, Dad?"

"I said I couldn't figure out how to turn off the computer," I replied rather sheepishly.

Chuckles, snickers and other unkind noises were my breakfast for the next 10 minutes as I sat thinking of how to get even.

Finally, one of them asked me, "Want to know how to turn it off, Dad?"

"I don't care if I ever find out or not."

"You have to click it to 'start'," she said.

"Right," I replied, "and the earth is flat."

"No," she said, "you really do."

"That's right," Ceci piped up.

"But it was *already* started," I stated.

"I know, but you still have to go to 'start' to turn it off," Ceci said with a smile.

"Why would I start something to turn it off, especially when it's already started?" I asked.

"That's just the way it works," my eight-year-old Hannah said rather condescendingly. "We'll just turn it on and off for you from now on, Dad."

As I said, it's hard to find something when you don't know what it is you're looking for. One of the reasons we have such a difficult time finding repentance is because *we don't know what we're looking for.*

In our search for revival, we must find repentance. Only when the Body of Christ fully comprehends the process of repentance—and lives accordingly—can the river of God flow through us in its pure state. Anything less causes the waters to be murky, polluted by our flesh. It is essential that repentance be worked out in our lives first in order for true revival—God's pure river of life—to flow through us and impact the world.

Repentance Means Never Having to Say You're Sorry...Again

Several years ago I was part of a well-organized evangelistic crusade called "I Found It." The only problem was most people didn't. Because the majority of those who prayed the "sinner's prayer" did not find true repentance, this campaign bore little lasting fruit.

So what is repentance, anyway? No, it isn't turning from sin and going another way. Nor does it mean remorse or sorrow for that sin. Not that these things aren't *related* to repentance—they are. But to limit our definition of repentance to these is to rob repentance of its incredible power to bring true transformation.

Because we don't really understand repentance, too many Christians repeatedly try to skip the *cause* and go straight to the *effect*. It doesn't work. This is the reason we so often "repent" of the same thing again and again. It's also why only 3 to 5 percent of our converts become true followers of Jesus Christ![1]

Let's figure out what we are looking for so we can find it.

Going His Way

A more accurate description of what we are trying to define might be the process of "turning our hearts," but because the word repentance is used so prevalently in the Body of Christ, I will call it the process of repentance. Properly defining three New Testament words will enable us to understand the process of repentance. These three words are "revelation," "repentance" and "turning."

"Revelation" comes from the word *apokalupsis* and means an "unveiling or uncovering"[2] (*kalupsis* meaning "cover or veil"; *apo* meaning "off or away"). It refers to God lifting the veil off the minds of humans in order to reveal information to them *from a divine perspective.*

"Repentance" is the Greek word *metanoia* and is literally defined as "knowing after"[3] (*meta* meaning "after"; *noeo* meaning "to know"). It is a new knowledge, perception or understanding that comes to us "after" our previous understanding. It is *a change of mind.*

The third word, "turning," is *epistrepho*. It means "to turn" and go a new direction, or "to return."[4] This is the *result* of revelation and repentance. Acts 3:19 says, "Repent therefore and return." Notice that repentance (*metanoia*) comes first, then the turning (*epistrepho*).

To better understand this verse, let's paraphrase it, "Repent, *in order that* you can return to God's way." Further clarification might be given by wording it this way: "Get God's knowledge or perspective of the situation—find out what He is saying—so you can turn and go His way."

Let's summarize the three concepts. Man needs an unveiling (revelation) to bring him a new understanding from God's perspective (repentance) so that he can turn and go God's way (turning).

> For years, the opening of "The Wide World of Sports" television program illustrated "the agony of defeat" with a painful ending to an attempted ski jump. The skier appeared in good form as he headed down the jump, but then, for no apparent reason, he tumbled head over heels off the side of the jump, bouncing off the supporting structure.
>
> What viewers didn't know was that he chose to fall rather than finish the jump. Why? As he explained later, the jump surface had become too fast, and midway down the ramp, he realized if he completed the jump, he would

land on the level ground, beyond the safe sloping landing area, which could have been fatal.

As it was, the skier suffered no more than a headache from the tumble.[5]

This man found repentance. Speeding down the jump, he received a revelation, bringing new understanding, and changed his direction. He decided the change was better than a fatal landing. His process of repentance saved his life. Ours can too, if we find it.

Human-Centered Repentance vs. God-Centered Repentance

A word that looks somewhat similar to the Greek word for repentance, but is very different in meaning, is *metamellomai*. This is what we usually have when we *think* we have true repentance. The word means "regret or remorse."[6] This *pain of mind*, or brokenness, is often the beginning of true repentance, when the consequences of our actions become real to us. Second Corinthians 7:8-11 speaks of this. Nevertheless, it is not yet full repentance and does not produce the desired change. Repentance is a *change* of mind—not just a *pain* of mind—resulting from a revelation brought by God. It is not simply a mental decision based on guilt.

The subtle danger of *metamellomai* is that its remorse is still rooted in *self*—the pain, shame or other negative consequences *I* experience as a result of *my* actions. It could be the loss of *my* family, the loss of *my* ministry, the shame *I* have to endure, or even the potential of *my* going to hell if *I* don't change. Zodhiates says it "means little more than a selfish dread of the consequence of what one has done."[7]

The fact that we feel bad about our sin is obviously not the problem. We should feel bad at times. But if it goes no further, feeling bad simply puts us in search of something to remedy *our* pain. This does not get us past the Fall, where humankind

105

became the center of its own universe and its motto in life became "What's in it for ME?" It is, in a very subtle way, still nothing more than humanism, or me-ism.

During construction of Emerson Hall at Harvard University, president Charles Eliot invited psychologist and philosopher William James to suggest a suitable inscription for the stone lintel over the doors of the new home of the philosophy department.

After some reflection, James sent Eliot a line from the Greek philosopher Protagoras: "Man is the measure of all things."

James never heard back from Eliot, so his curiosity was piqued when he spotted artisans working on a scaffold hidden by a canvas. One morning the scaffold and canvas were gone. The inscription? "What is man that thou art mindful of him?"

Eliot had replaced James's suggestion with words from the psalmist. Between these two lines lies the great distance between the God-centered and the human-centered points of view.[8]

Human-centered repentance makes humankind and its pain or loss the measuring point; true repentance is God-centered.

When the gospel is presented to a sinner, or a believer is repentant of sin, the emphasis should not be upon the person's benefit. This always perverts the outcome. The issue is we have sinned against a holy God. Nothing and no one else can take center stage, which is why David said, when he found true repentance after his sin with Bathsheba, "Against Thee, Thee only, I have sinned" (Ps. 51:4).

I used to be bothered by this statement—I even disputed it with the Lord. I told Him David had sinned against his wife, the nation Israel, the noble Uriah (Bathsheba's husband and one of David's mighty men) and the Lord his God. Such an assertion may be accurate in a natural sense, and restitution may be appropriate at times, but that is not the issue where true repentance is concerned. God and God alone is the issue. If this were not so, restitution alone would bring forgiveness from God when we sin against others. Of course, we know it does not. David found true repentance when he saw his condition from God's perspective and confessed his sin.

Even the "broken and contrite heart" (Ps. 51:17) that David said pleased the Lord would not have been enough by itself. Many people have a broken or contrite heart, yet never come to forgiveness—much less transformation. Judas is probably the best-known example of this. The Bible says he experienced great remorse (*metamellomai*—see Matt. 27:3). He gave the 30 pieces of silver back and hung himself. There is no record, however, of Judas receiving forgiveness. He didn't find repentance.

Esau couldn't find it either. "He found no place for repentance, though he sought for it with tears" (Heb. 12:17). Again, regret or sorrow is not the same as repentance. And they do not bring forgiveness to us.

All three words—this entire concept of repentance—are linked to the Fall of humankind and the tree of the knowledge of good and evil. If not understood in this context, we have not fully comprehended them.

The Self-Exaltation of Humankind

When Adam and Eve disobeyed and partook of the forbidden tree, they were exalting themselves—becoming "like God" (Gen. 3:5)—and exalting their own wisdom and knowledge. They were choosing their knowledge over His. When this happened a veiling (*kalupto*) of their minds to God's truth occurred (see 2 Cor. 4:3). Exalting their own knowledge blinded them to God's.

> In whose case the god of this world has *blinded* the minds of the unbelieving, that they might not see the light of the gospel of the glory of Christ, who is the image of God (2 Cor. 4:4, italics mine).

The Greek word for blinded in this verse (*tuphloo*) conveys the concept of a smoke screen and carries the meaning of self-exaltation or pride.[9] Simply put, men and women have smoke screens that keep them blinded or veiled from the truth.

—

Why does it seem more reasonable to believe that everything evolved from a big bang than to believe it was created by a loving God?

—

First Corinthians 2:14 states the things of God are "foolish" (*moria*) to "natural man." The word *moria* means literally "moronish."[10] Until the veil is lifted (revelation), the things of God will seem ridiculous to humankind.

The natural mind struggles with concepts such as the virgin birth, the incarnation of Christ, the Resurrection, miracles, even a supernatural Creation. It seems more reasonable to humankind to believe that everything evolved from a big bang than to believe it was created by a loving God. If humans cannot figure out and explain something rationally, they have great difficulty accepting it. This is because of the effects of the Fall.

God intended that we be spiritually controlled, not mind-controlled. The Greek word for a spiritual person is *pneumatikos*, coming from the word *pneuma* which means spirit. It refers to one controlled, influenced or motivated by the spirit. Humankind lost this ability at the Fall. A reversal took place in the Garden—the soul took dominance. But Christ came to restore life to God's pattern: walking according to the spirit.

The phrase "natural man" comes from *psuchikos*, the root word of which is *psuche*, meaning the soul (the mind, emotions and will). Translated literally, *psuchikos* is a soulish or soul-motivated and controlled person; one who operates not from the spirit, but the soul, the *psuche*. And because the soul chose to exalt itself above God and His knowledge, humankind's ability to see truth from God's perspective was severely damaged. The veil descended and blindness came.

The repentance process reverses this state of affairs for us. Because of this veiling (*kalupsis*) and blinding, humankind needed an unveiling (*apokalupsis*—revelation) to bring them a new knowledge from God (*metanoia*—repentance), thus enabling them to turn and go God's way (*epistrepho*—turn or return) again.

God is continuously—at times more intensely than others—trying to enlighten us to His way of thinking so we can continually walk His way. When turning is required—adjustments, change—we must do it. From this definition we can see that repentance does not necessarily have to involve sin. Anytime He adjusts us to His way of thinking through a revelation of the Holy Spirit, which should happen regularly, this is repentance. We can then turn and go His way. My entire lifestyle should be one of repentance as I continually learn His ways. This is why we can live a life of repentance without being plagued by condemnation or a guilt complex.

It Takes Time to Turn the Titanic Around

Sometimes we think up is down and down is up. Life can be confusing.

> Some years ago a speedboat driver who had survived a racing accident described what had happened. He said he had been at near-top speeds when his boat veered slightly and hit a wave at a dangerous angle. The combined force of his speed and the size and angle of the wave sent the boat spinning crazily into the air. He was thrown from his seat and propelled deeply into the water—so deep, in fact, that he had no idea which direction the surface was. He had to remain calm and wait for the buoyancy of his life vest to begin pulling him up. Once he discovered which way was up, he could swim for the surface.[11]

If we will wait on Him, God's gentle tug will pull us in the right direction. Our "life vest" may be the Word, another Christian or an inner witness from the Holy Spirit. But the key is to allow Him to show us His way...to find repentance.

> Trust in the Lord with all thine heart; and lean not unto thine own understanding. In all thy ways acknowledge him, and he shall direct thy paths (Prov. 3:5,6, *KJV*).

I refer to all of this as the *process* of repentance because it usually comes over a period of time, as we *gradually* are transformed into His way of thinking. In most cases, the course of our ships cannot be changed instantaneously. We aren't made to facilitate a sudden change of direction; we would capsize. When the unveiling happens and revelation finally breaks in on us, it often seems to have happened suddenly. But in reality, a series of smaller unveilings—increments of truth breaking through, seeds of God's word being planted—have likely led up to the "sudden" revelation.

Obviously, the larger the ship and the farther off course, the longer the adjustment period. Thus it is often a lengthy process to bring repentance—God's new knowledge or way of thinking—to the Church as a whole.

"Please Co Back to Your Seat, You're Not Ready Yet"

Though true repentance and turning bring forgiveness, God's goal is much loftier than this. He's shooting for *transformation*. When we receive revelation from Him, enabling us to see our conditions from His perspective, this unveiling also reveals His grace and redemption to us. We see our need, but we also see His provision. The exposing and humbling of self with the counteraction of God being exalted allows the release of grace. His grace then empowers and enables us to *effectively* "turn and go the other way."

This is why the great evangelist Charles Finney would often preach four, five or more nights before he gave the first altar call during his crusades. He allowed time for this process of repentance to occur. Finney was actually known to have grown men run to the altar weeping during a message and he would tell them, "Please go back to your seat, you're not ready yet." This is also why he had 97 percent of his converts become true followers of Christ compared to our 3 to 5 percent today.

The failure to place many of our biblical truths—especially the process of repentance—in the context of the Fall, where humankind exalted itself and came out from under God's rule, has been very costly. Anything associated with forgiveness, grace and transformation that isn't understood through this is deficient. The implications of the Fall—humankind's exaltation and rebellion—are the very reasons the absolute first criteria for receiving grace is to humble one's self (see Jas. 4:6, 1 Pet. 5:5). The *lordship* of Jesus becomes of paramount importance when this is clearly understood. If He does not truly become Lord in a person's life, then the fruit of rebellion and self-exaltation will continue there. When our gospel fails here, it has failed absolutely.

We have removed "the offence of the Cross" (Gal. 5:11, *KJV*) and in so doing we have removed the power of the gospel to transform. Jesus didn't come to appease self but, on the contrary, "commandeth all men every where to repent" (Acts 17:30, *KJV*).

A "What's in it for me?" gospel has taken center stage in our country. When we preach a humanistic (man at the center) gospel, we produce humanistic, self-centered converts. How could a humanistic gospel that never gets self to the Cross, but instead makes the appeal to the self's motivation, do anything else? Preach to people of the blessings, and they love it. Ask for a little sacrifice, and they quickly disappear. Little if anything is said about taking up and living at the Cross *daily*. Most Americans don't even know what it means. "Jesus paid it all so I can be happy." This is really all that matters to them.

Only 3 to 5 percent of the people who donate money to a church tithe their income.[12] Only 60 percent attend a church service weekly. Most never pray or spend time in the Word of God—unless *they* need or want something. The average Christian family of four in America today gives $20.80 a year toward foreign missions. The Church of America spends $5 billion annually on new religious buildings, while investing $1 million a year to

—

God's holy hammer of truth is about to descend on America! It would be far wiser for us to fall on the Rock before He falls on us.

≈

reach the unreached with the gospel. That's a ratio of 5000 to 1— buildings over people, comfort over commission.[13] There is very little concern for the cause of Christ.

Discipleship, commitment, selfless giving and living, sacrifice for our commission and other spiritual disciplines don't stand a chance with this anemic gospel. It is costless, causeless Christianity at its worst, and America is inundated with it! God's holy hammer of truth is about to descend on it with incredible tenaciousness! It would be far wiser for us to fall on the Rock before He falls on us (see Matt. 21:44). We must do it now.

Dr. George Sweeting wrote in *Special Sermons for Special Days*:

Several years ago our family visited Niagara Falls. It was spring, and ice was rushing down the river. As I viewed the large blocks of ice flowing toward the falls, I could see that there were carcasses of dead fish embedded in the ice. Gulls by the score were riding down the river feeding on the fish. As they came to the brink of the falls, their wings would go out, and they would escape from the falls.

I watched one gull which seemed to delay and wondered when it would leave. It was engrossed in the carcass of a fish, and when it finally came to the brink of the falls, out went its powerful wings. The bird flapped and flapped and even lifted the ice out of the water, and I thought it would escape. But it had delayed too long so that its claws had frozen into the ice. The weight of the ice was too great, and the gull plunged into the abyss.

As Sweeting observed, "Oh, the danger of delay!"[14]

Transformation Can Only Be Found at the Cross

The irony is we have taken God's instrument of death for the exalted self-life—the Cross—and made it an instrument of blessing to that life. Our error actually strengthens the problem—the self. God doesn't want to bless self; He wants it dead. One of the greatest heresies we could preach is that Jesus went to the Cross so we wouldn't have to. This is true in a physical sense but not spiritually. Jesus actually went to the Cross so we *could*, bringing the death of the old man. Christ said, "If anyone wishes to come after Me, let him deny himself, and take up his cross daily, and follow Me" (Luke 9:23). The Cross is where *we* must die *daily*. We have missed this pitifully.

The Cross is not just something to wear around our necks; it is supposed to wear us. Consider the fact that much of the time when Jesus mentioned going to the Cross, He added the fact that we, too, must go there (see Matt. 16:21-26; Mark 8:31-38; Luke 9:22-27; John 12:23-26). More than just a symbolic identification with Him—don't disarm it with such a powerless interpretation—He speaks of a very real laying down of our lives.

When we're told to lay down our *lives* in the New Testament, it is referring to the exalted self-life that came at the Fall. The word used is *psuche*. As I mentioned, this is also the word for soul—that which contains the mind, emotions and will. Therefore, when we're commanded to lay down our lives, we're being told to lay down the "life" that is rooted in the exalted soul of humankind—that which causes rebellion, independence and self-exaltation. Again, if we don't bring this to the Cross and find true repentance, there will be no transformation.

113

"Well, What's the Good News?"

In summary, we have basically missed the mark with our approach to repentance in three ways. First, we have defined it as "turning and going the other way" which jumps to the effect, missing the cause.

Secondly, we have thought of it as remorse or being sorry for our sins. This stops short of true repentance and often focuses the attention back on self, as it seeks to find a way out of its dilemma. Remorse sometimes leads to and is often the result of genuine repentance, but is not to be confused with it.

Third is the salesman approach—sadly the most destructive and the area in which we have transgressed the most. We try to "sell" Jesus based on His many wonderful benefits. Perhaps "sell" isn't the best word, because there is certainly no price for the sinner to pay; Jesus paid it all. What remains, then, is for them to cash in on all the benefits. Going to heaven when they die is just the icing on the cake. This is nothing more than an appeal to the exalted self-life, which remains on the throne asking, "What's in it for me?"

Paul said, "My speech and my preaching was not with enticing words" (1 Cor. 2:4, *KJV*). The truth is we're not salesmen, nor is our gospel some smorgasbord of goodies. Jesus doesn't invite us to "give Me a try." On the contrary, He *commands*, "Take up your cross. Follow Me!"

Our efforts at outreach have become too watered down. This almost always happens during these seasons when God is working more *in* us than *through* us. Because we don't understand the season, we try anything to produce outward growth. Sales and marketing approaches and watered-down gospels become the order of the day—anything to see a little fruit.

When Lloyd C. Douglas, author of *The Robe* and other novels, was a university student, he lived in a boarding house, says Maxie Dunnam in *Jesus' Claims—Our Promises*. Downstairs on the first floor was an elderly, retired music teacher, now infirm and unable to leave the apartment.

Douglas said that every morning they had a ritual they

would go through together. He would come down the steps, open the old man's door, and ask, "Well, what's the good news?"

The old man would pick up his tuning fork, tap it on the side of his wheelchair, and say, "That's Middle C! It was middle C yesterday; it will be middle C tomorrow; it will be middle C a thousand years from now. The tenor upstairs sings flat, the piano across the hall is out of tune, but my friend, *that* is middle C!"

The old man had discovered one thing upon which he could depend, one constant reality in his life.[15]

The true gospel message never changes. It included the Cross yesterday; it will include the Cross tomorrow; it will include the Cross a thousand years from now. We may not like it. The world certainly doesn't. But, my friends, the true gospel includes the Cross—our Cross!

In contrast to these false approaches, true biblical repentance—a new knowledge causing us to see our situations from God's perspective—is the result of divine revelation. This breaks the back of exalted self, getting it to the Cross, resulting in transformation and a supernatural ability to turn.

What has this to do with harvest and the river? Everything! The process of revival begins with the process of repentance. And where revival is concerned, it must begin with the Church, then spread to the world. The inpouring *to* us precedes the outpouring *through* us. Revival in the Church will precede revival in the world. He must re*vive* us before He can *vive* through us.

God is bringing to us an awareness of our weaknesses so He can fill them with His strength (see 2 Cor. 12:9). *"He has torn us, but He will heal us"* (Hos. 6:1, italics mine). He is revealing to us a "new knowledge" in many areas of our lives so we can turn and go His way. The result will be vessels "for honor, sanctified, useful to the Master" (2 Tim. 2:21).

Those who think as He does can be trusted with His gifts and anointings. These blessings will no longer be prostituted for personal gain, but will be cast as crowns at His feet. He will increase; we will decrease (see John 3:30).

The result will be life to the world. The *times of refreshing* will come from His presence (see Acts 3:19). The fallow ground will have been broken, righteousness will be rained upon us (see Hos. 10:12), and the river will flow.

I'm still looking for that computer switch, but I found repentance.

Notes

1. These figures were given to me in 1984 at Christ for the Nations Institute. I cannot imagine they have changed much as no greater percentage of Americans attend church regularly now then at that time.
2. Spiros Zodhiates, *Hebrew-Greek Key Study Bible—New American Standard* (Chattanooga: AMG Publishers, 1984; revised edition, 1990), p. 1809.
3. Ibid., p. 1856.
4. Ibid., p. 1834.
5. Craig Brian Larson, *Illustrations for Preaching and Teaching* (Grand Rapids: Baker Books, 1993), p. 21.
6. Zodhiates, *Hebrew-Greek Key Study Bible—New American Standard*, p. 1856.
7. Ibid., p. 1856.
8. Edward K. Rowell, *Fresh Illustrations for Preaching and Teaching* (Grand Rapids: Baker Books, 1997), p. 90.
9. James Strong, *The New Strong's Exhaustive Concordance of the Bible* (Nashville: Thomas Nelson Publishers, 1990), ref. no. 5186.
10. Zodiates, *Hebrew-Greek Key Study Bible—New American Standard*, p. 1858.
11. Larson, *Illustrations for Preaching and Teaching*, p. 174.
12. George Barna, *How to Increase Giving in Your Church* (Ventura: Regal Books, 1997), p. 20.
13. David Barrett, *Our Globe and How to Reach It* (Birmingham: New Hope Publishing, 1991).
14. Larson, *Illustrations for Preaching and Teaching*, p. 180.
15. Ibid., p. 27.

CHAPTER SEVEN

Not REALLY Lost

Have you ever been lost? I have. Well, not *really* lost. I'm a man, you understand. We don't get lost; we simply drive around for hours trying to make others believe we are. It's a game. After a few hours we stop to "use the restroom" and very discreetly check with someone else to confirm that we're not *really* lost.

"Yep, right on target," we declare to our passengers. "All we do is...." The most I've not *really* been lost is about 90 miles.

I recall the time I wasn't *really* lost in the woods. I was hunting in an area of Colorado that was new to me. We arrived at our cabin late in the afternoon and I decided to take advantage of the last couple hours of daylight. *I'll just go scout around a little,* I thought. *This will give me a slight advantage in the morning. And who knows, I might even get lucky and see an elk. Better take my gun.*

I scouted around about 20 minutes too long. This meant a lengthy walk back to the cabin in the dark. No problem. I had my flashlight, compass and survival gear. I wasn't scared. That's why I whistled and hummed as I walked. I always whistle and hum in a woods at night when I'm not *really* lost and not *really* scared.

Somewhere I missed a turn. Things look different going the opposite direction, especially in the dark.

Nothing jump-starts the imagination like being alone and lost—well, not *really* lost—in an unknown woods at night. (Not that I was scared, you understand.) Creatures I don't even believe in live in unknown woods at night. I heard noises that were downright *weird*. I also walked past approximately 10 mountain lions and five bears. Luckily, they heard me whistling, detected my confidence and ran off. It helps to be smarter than they are.

In times like these, at some point the mind begins to think crazy thoughts and ask strange questions. *I know all elk are supposed to be vegetarians, but I wonder if some are really meat eaters?* I recall thinking. *They don't have deductive reasoning as we humans, but could they possibly know why I'm out here?*

"Naw!" I heard myself say out loud.

Then for some unknown reason I also heard myself say very loudly, "Sure is a great night for a walk. I hope no elk think I've been hunting them."

Suddenly something jumped near the trail. Limbs and branches cracked and the ground shook as something sounding like a horse rumbled through the night. After I set a new record for the 400-meter dash, I slowed down to 50 mph and congratulated myself for having the calmness to take advantage of this time alone to enjoy some jogging. If you're going to be *almost* but not *really* lost in the woods, you might as well get in a little aerobic exercise.

"Most guys would never think of that," I bragged to myself. "They'd be too scared." Finally I came to the main road. I was only a mile or two south of where I wanted to be. *Not bad*, I thought.

As I approached the cabin my concerned buddies were outside waiting for me. "We were starting to get worried," they said. "Were you lost?"

"Not really," I replied.

"Probably just wanted a little exercise, right?" they remarked in a matter-of-fact manner. Guys understand things like this.

We in the Body of Christ don't *really* get off course. We just wander around exercising in the dark. Yeah, right! The reality of our denial is often lost to us. (Think about it—it'll come.)

No one is perfect, and all have blind spots. We lose our bearings from time to time and need directional adjustments. Not only do we get off course individually, but movements and organizations do as well. We are very human. Someone once said that people are like most folks.

Five Ways to Get Lost

We can find examples of movements needing adjustment to God's way of thinking (repentance) in the charismatic and Jesus movements of the '60s and '70s. Because I am a product of these, and would be considered a charismatic by many, I can "pick on us" without my comments being of a critical nature. Also, having been a participant, I know them better than I do other movements or organizations.

In the next two chapters, I will discuss five failures which I believe short-circuited these moves of God, causing them to fall short of all He wanted to accomplish through them. Though applied to these two movements in particular, they are common mistakes and therefore valid for all. My purpose in rehashing these errors is to help us preserve this next wave of revival and keep it from getting off course.

I do not mean to imply these movements were total failures; though this is a critique of sorts, it is not meant to be critical. God did accomplish much through these particular flows of the river. Through them, thousands were saved and filled with the Holy Spirit; the Jesus movement impacted a very hopeless generation; the teaching office of Ephesians 4:11 was restored to the Church; worship matured immensely; and other blessings were released as well. As mentioned, I personally was touched in a major way and am, to one degree or another, a product of these particular renewals.

In spite of the blessings, however, the five weaknesses I want to discuss were very serious. Of course, there may have been more, but these stand out to me. (Incidentally, I'm giving them to you alliteratively, which those of you schooled in the finer points of preaching know increases the anointing level significantly. Hallelujah for honed, heavenly homiletics!)

119

Haste Without Heart

The first of these undermining flaws I call *haste without heart*.
The biblical passage which illustrates this condition is 2 Samuel
18:19-33. The setting is the death of Absalom, David's son who had
stolen the throne from him for a short while.

> Then Ahimaaz the son of Zadok said, "Please let me run
> and bring the king news that the Lord has freed him from
> the hand of his enemies."
>
> But Joab said to him, "You are not the man to carry news
> this day, but you shall carry news another day; however, you
> shall carry no news today *because the king's son is dead.*"
> Then Joab said to the Cushite, "Go, tell the king what you
> have seen." So the Cushite bowed to Joab and ran.
>
> Now Ahimaaz the son of Zadok said once more to
> Joab, "But whatever happens, please let me also run after
> the Cushite."
>
> And Joab said, "Why would you run, my son, since *you
> will have no reward for going?*"
>
> "But whatever happens," he said, "I will run."
>
> So he said to him, "Run." Then Ahimaaz ran by way of
> the plain and passed up the Cushite.
>
> Now David was sitting between the two gates; and the
> watchman went up to the roof of the gate by the wall, and
> raised his eyes and looked, and behold, a man running by
> himself. And the watchman called and told the king. And
> the king said, "If he is by himself there is good news in his
> mouth." And he came nearer and nearer.
>
> Then the watchman saw another man running; and the
> watchman called to the gatekeeper and said, "Behold,
> another man running by himself."
>
> And the king said, "This one also is bringing good
> news."
>
> And the watchman said, "I think the running of the first
> one is like the running of Ahimaaz the son of Zadok."

And the king said, "This is a good man and comes with good news."

And Ahimaaz called and said to the king, "All is well." And he prostrated himself before the king with his face to the ground. And he said, "Blessed is the Lord your God, who has delivered up the men who lifted their hands against my lord the king,"

And the king said, "Is it well with the young man Absalom?"

And Ahimaaz answered, "When Joab sent the king's servant, and your servant, I saw a great tumult, but *I did not know* what it was."

Then the king said, "Turn aside and stand here." So he turned aside and stood still.

And behold, the Cushite arrived, and the Cushite said, "Let my lord the king receive good news, for the Lord has freed you this day from the hand of all those who rose up against you."

Then the king said to the Cushite, "Is it well with the young man Absalom?"

And the Cushite answered, "Let the enemies of my lord the king, and all who rise up against you for evil, be as that young man!"

And *the king was deeply moved and went up to the chamber over the gate and wept.* And thus he said as he walked, "O my son Absalom, my son, my son Absalom! Would I had died instead of you, O Absalom, my son, my son!" (italics mine).

Ahimaaz was very fast. He started last but arrived first. He ran in vain, however—"you will have no reward for going" (v. 22)— because he didn't have the complete message. And he did not have the entire message because *he didn't identify with the king's heart.* David had not only defeated an enemy, he had lost a son. Ahimaaz eventually stepped aside in ignorance, insignificance and embarrassment as a nameless individual took center stage and delivered the complete message.

Our message will always in some way be deficient if it isn't related to the King's heart. I'm speaking, of course, of God our King—Jesus, our heavenly Father, and the Holy Spirit. The pleasure of the Father is—and must remain—the ultimate goal of our

—

Persistent, hanging-in-there, long-term building should receive more honor than something that springs up quickly. Sadly, it does not.

—

running. The glory and exaltation of the Son must be our chief aim. His passion and priority of harvesting sons and daughters into the family must become ours.

Why Are We Running?

This begs the question of our *motives* for service. Why are we running? Why are we building, seeking revival? Is it for personal fulfillment, fame, glory, self-aggrandizement, to make a name for ourselves? Or are we, as the Cushite in this passage, content to remain nameless? Is it for advancement, a position? Is it to display our gifts, our speed? Are we looking to build something big?

Some are motivated by the needs of people. This seems noble, but Jesus was never dictated to by the needs of those He ministered to, only by the will of the Father. "Need motivation" will cause us to run for people's benefit, not God's. It will also wear us out, as we are *driven* by the incredible need of the human race.

Still others run for the pure excitement of running. I agree we should enjoy the journey, but we aren't to run for the thrill of it. In Philippians 3:14, Paul said, "I press *toward the mark*" (*KJV*, italics mine). His goal, or mark as he called it, was clear.

In verse 12 he said, "I press on in order that I may lay hold of that for which also I was laid hold of by Christ Jesus" (*NASB*).

In 1 Corinthians 9:24, he urges us, "Run in such a way that you may win." Our reason for running must be Him. Winning is when we accomplish Christ's purpose.

The Gift Mentality

Unfortunately, the charismatic movement, as positive as it was, gave us a *gift mentality*: Run on the strength of your gift. The very word "charismatic" means grace *gifts*. This led to a *performance mentality*: run to set records, to be first, to be the best, to be the biggest. Go for the gold! "Build 'em big and build 'em fast!" became the mind-set. Overnight sensations were, and in many ways still are, the order of the day. *There is nothing biblical about this mind-set!* Persistent, progressive, hanging-in-there, long-term building should receive more honor than something that springs up quickly. Sadly, it does not. Far more character is needed to build a work or ministry over a lengthy time than to enjoy something which happens quickly.

One of the basic problems with this philosophy, aside from pride and self-exaltation, is that if *any* part of our vision (which becomes the goal of running) is born of *ambition* rather than *God's heart,* we soon are running for *self,* not the King. Zeal that was originally to do something *for God* becomes a zeal *to remain successful.* This can be so subtle, it frequently happens without our even realizing it.

Contrary to what is often taught—and usually done—*vision must never be our starting place.* Vision *born of God's heart* must be where we begin. In my younger days it was hammered into me by many: "Get a vision." Again and again, I heard it. They should have been saying, "Find God's heart. Seek His face."

The questions we must continually ask ourselves are, How well do I understand and relate to the King's heart in this matter? Is it my motive for running? For building? Was His heart the birthplace of my vision?

The question is *not,* How fast or gifted am I? *Never* does this validate our running! God's pattern of service is always in this order:

1. He matures us into His character.
2. He entrusts us with His heart.

3. He directs us with His vision.
4. He enables us with His anointing and provision.
5. He releases us to minister our gifts to accomplish and fulfill.

Holy Hubert

A gentleman used greatly by God in the early days of the charismatic movement exemplifies this principle. He was a part of a move of the Holy Spirit that was eventually called the Jesus movement. This movement was used by God to bring thousands of drug-bound, sexually perverted, disillusioned and hopeless young people into the kingdom of God. His name was Hubert Lindsay, but he became known as "Holy Hubert."

Like King David, who wasn't called by his father to the potential king lineup, nothing about Holy Hubert's appearance or personality caused him to stand apart. He was short, didn't have much charisma, was even a little "different" than the socially accepted norm.

I once had the privilege of hearing Mr. Lindsay speak. He told of his calling to and ministry at the University of Southern California at Berkeley. The people who were there that day may remember what he said about the miracles and the salvations. They may recall the humor with which it was told. They had laughed, cheered and applauded. What I fear may have been missed, however, was a passing comment Holy Hubert made about how the ministry was birthed.

"I became so burdened for this generation," he said, "that I would walk the streets of the campus—sometimes all night long—weeping and interceding for those kids. I pled with God to give me those young people." God broke his heart for a generation.

The Lord answered his cry *because it was His own* and gave him a generation. Church historians agree that the Jesus movement was of extreme significance in the renewal of the '60s and '70s. And when tracing the roots of the Jesus movement, one invariably ends up at Berkeley and Holy Hubert Lindsay.

His burden cost him dearly, however. His broken heart led to broken bones—not to a nice salary or a large congregation. Lindsay and his wife were beaten on numerous occasions, stabbed, mocked and ridiculed as they preached the gospel on campus. She eventually suffered brain damage, and Holy Hubert lost his sight due to the beatings. As the Apostle Paul, they bore on their bodies the marks of the Lord Jesus (see Gal. 6:17).

The Lindsays picture for us the principle of starting, not with a vision, ministry or gifts, but with the heart of God concerning a particular need—and allowing that to become the motivating reason for ministry. This releases the river in a pure form, keeping it free of the debris of pride and selfish motivation.

Our failure to do this has resulted in a generation of believers who believe gifting qualifies a person for ministry. We allowed ourselves to bypass character and other heart issues in these movements. God's heart was replaced by other priorities and motivations, which inevitably led to us building our own kingdoms. A cooperative heart (God's) was superseded by a competitive heart (humankind's). Travailing, agonizing prayer was replaced by the strength of our gifts. Last, and probably most tragic, success was measured not by how well we knew the Father, but by how well-known we were.

Push has come to shove, Ahimaaz has passed the Cushite, and the Father is weeping. Repentance must come. We need an alignment. Our fast moving, state-of-the-art churches are pulling to the right and left. Things are out of balance. We have compensated for our ignorance with speed, and we are out of control. *Please, Lord, help us see this situation from Your perspective. Give us repentance. We must have an unveiling. Deliver us from ourselves!*

Speed Without Seasoned Skill

The second weakness of these movements, one to which we are all susceptible, was *speed without seasoned skill*. This is illustrated in 2 Samuel 2:18-23:

Now the three sons of Zeruiah were there, Joab and
Abishai and Asahel; and Asahel was as swift-footed as one
of the gazelles which is in the field. And Asahel pursued
Abner and did not turn to the right or to the left from following Abner.

Then Abner looked behind him and said, "Is that you,
Asahel?"

And he answered, "It is I."

So Abner said to him, "Turn to your right or to your
left, and take hold of one of the young men for yourself,
and take for yourself his spoil."

But Asahel was not willing to turn aside from following him.

And Abner repeated again to Asahel, "Turn aside from
following me. Why should I strike you to the ground?
How then could I lift up my face to your brother Joab?"

However, he refused to turn aside; therefore Abner
struck him in the belly with the butt end of the spear, so
that the spear came out at his back. And he fell there and
died on the spot. And it came about that all who came to
the place where Asahel had fallen and died, stood still.

Though similar to *haste without heart*, this is different.
Whereas the first point relates to our *motives*, this weakness
speaks of our *maturity levels*: training, preparation, wisdom and
understanding. So far as we know, Asahel's motives were fine. He
simply didn't have the necessary wisdom for the battle. Ahimaaz
ran for the *wrong reasons*; Asahel ran *prematurely*.

A wise person counts the cost before going to war and asks,
"Do I have what it requires to win?" Before building, it is prudent
to ask, "Do I have the necessary resources to finish this task?"

From New Year's resolutions and our repeated attempts to
become more spiritually disciplined to building churches and
growing ministries, many of us start projects well but finish
poorly. I've seen too many ministries explode quickly into big
organizations but eventually fail through compromise or poor

planning. It's not how we start the race but how we finish that matters the most.

At 7 P.M. on October 20, 1968, a few thousand spectators remained in the Mexico City Olympic Stadium. It was cool and dark. The last of the marathon runners, each exhausted, were being carried off to first-aid stations. More than an hour earlier, Mamo Wolde of Ethiopia—looking as fresh as when he started the race—crossed the finish line, the winner of the 26-mile, 385-yard event.

As the remaining spectators prepared to leave, those sitting near the marathon gates suddenly heard the sound of sirens and police whistles. All eyes turned to the gate. A lone figure wearing number 36 and the colors of Tanzania entered the stadium. His name was John Stephen Akhwari. He was the last man to finish the marathon. He had fallen during the race and injured his knee and ankle. Now, with his leg bloodied and bandaged, he grimaced with each hobbling step around the 400-meter track.

The spectators rose and applauded him. After crossing the finish line, Akhwari slowly walked off the field. Later, a reporter asked Akhwari the question on everyone's mind: "Why did you continue to race after you were so badly injured?"

He replied, "My country did not send me 7,000 miles to start the race. They sent me 7,000 miles to finish it."

"Let us run with perseverance the race marked out for us" (Heb. 12:1).[1]

God didn't call us to *start* a race; He called us to *finish* it.

In running the spiritual race of life, zeal alone is not enough. Zeal often *generates*, but seldom *sustains*. Good intentions are not enough—it's *not* just the thought that counts. Contrary to popular belief, ignorance is not bliss. A great vision, talent, gifts, abilities, speed—none are sufficient for producing the kind of fruit God wants.

The charismatic movement, in spite of its strengths and blessings, in many ways glorified the wrong requirements for our running. Much of the error was directly related to impatience—

Nowhere in the Scriptures will you
find speed or size to be the
criteria for success or greatness.

"now-ism." Speed and gifting, not wisdom and character, were
the main criteria for ministry. The following tendencies manifested themselves in the movement:

- Knowledge was glorified over wisdom.
- Revelation was exalted over sound doctrine.
- Reaping was given priority over sowing.
- The works of God replaced the ways of God.
- Gifts and charisma took precedence over experience
  and understanding.
- Instant gratification replaced endurance.
- Formulas and how-to's replaced waiting on God.
- Church growth and success seminars replaced prayer
  meetings and prayer watches.
- Seasoning, training and wisdom were neglected for the
  sake of speed.
- Action took priority over accountability—the ends
  began to justify the means.
- Fathers without enough fire and speed were rejected—
  along with their wisdom—and our peers became our
  counselors. Fire counseled fire! The results? Fireworks!
  The problem? After a few bright flashes, it was all over.

Speed and size spelled success. An instant-gratification, buy-
now/pay-later, live-for-today, humanistic world somehow suc-
ceeded in conforming much of the Church to its ways.

Phrases such as "fastest growing" and "one of the largest" became an absolute curse to the Body of Christ, a curse which continues to operate. Inherent in them are wrong motivation, a deficient understanding of God, the wounding of others and the propagating of a competitive spirit. We not only shoot our wounded in the Body of Christ, we often do the wounding with our carnal mind-sets. Nowhere in the Scriptures will you find speed or size to be the criteria for success or greatness. Yet they take center stage in our Christian culture. I fear this has done much more damage than we realize. When our standard of judgment is distorted, the goal invariably goes amiss also.

Enough time has passed that it is now possible to judge the fruit of this distortion of God's ways. I'm not aware of a city in America that has experienced genuine revival as a result of one of the fastest-growing or largest churches. In spite of our supposed growth and the many megachurches that now exist, there is not a greater percentage of Americans attending church today than there was 20 years ago. Of the purported growth, 90 percent has been from transfers, not conversions. Unlike His Church, I don't think God is very impressed with our results. He probably spends a great deal of time mourning the Asahels who have been run through with the enemy's spear and grieving over the competitive spirit that permeates the Body of Christ.

Whereas our penchant for size and speed have failed to reach our cities for Christ, I read of a poor but wise man who delivered an entire city through his wisdom (see Eccles. 9:15). The same passage says, "wisdom is better than strength" (v. 16) and "wisdom is better than weapons of war" (v. 18).

The Need for Maturity

We spoke of the five biblical stages of Christian growth in chapter four. In these progressive levels of maturity, a person was not considered qualified until reaching the fourth position, *huios*. At this point there was a *huiothesia*, the placing (*thesia*) into sonship (*huios*). (The issue here isn't gender, but maturity.) A fully matured son was considered adequately prepared to be on his

129

own, to function out from under teachers and trainers. The *huio-thesia* usually took place at around 30 years of age.

This is what happened at Christ's baptism. In a *huiothesia* ceremony, the instructor, called in that day a *pedagogue*, presented the mature son to the father. The father would then publicly announce, "This is my beloved *son*, in whom I am well pleased." Not a *child*, but now a *son*. When Christ was baptized, the Father publicly spoke those words (see Matt. 3:17).

Then, and only then, was Christ released to begin ministry. He could then be trusted to fully, and without exception, follow the will and ways of the Father. He had "become strong, increasing in wisdom" (Luke 2:40) and "learned obedience" (Heb. 5:8). Don't recoil at that—let Him be human. His release, His *huiothesia*, was based on wisdom and character, not His gifts.

We have not understood this in the Church. We choose and release our leaders based on gifting. We assign novices—*nepioses, paidions and teknons*, stages 1-3 of Christian maturity—to run churches, ministries and Sunday Schools and sit on deacon boards and committees. And we wonder why the Body of Christ is in such a mess. Why don't we see more fruit? More people saved? More purity? More depth of commitment? Longer lasting moves of the Spirit?

Because of our emphasis on *speed without seasoned skill*, we have been building without character, without much depth, with a lot of debt and without sufficient foundations to support our structures. We have broken the rules, but still want to win the war. Instead many, like Asahel, have been speared by the enemy. Casualties abound. And they will continue until we begin to judge by God's standards, not our own.

Let us *press on to maturity* as we prepare for this great river outpouring. Anything less is suicidal.

Sensationalism Without Substance

The third problem pervading the Jesus and charismatic movements—and, indeed, the modern Church—was *sensationalism without substance*. Revelation 3:1,2 says of the church at Sardis,

"You have a name that you are alive, but you are dead. Wake up, and strengthen the things that remain, which were about to die."

This church had obviously been strong at one point and continued to have a reputation of being alive. God, however, looked at the heart of the church and saw its true condition. The fact that these people had a name declaring they were alive tells us they were still "doing the right things." The church looked good, looked alive. In reality, however, it was dead.

The inevitable result of points one and two, this problem speaks of our *methods*. It represents building, not on the anointing of the Holy Spirit, but on formulas, hype, sensationalism, big

———

An overemphasis on power and miracles
always leads to sensationalism and,
ultimately, a decrease in power.

———

names, miracles, the gifts of the Spirit, innovation—anything that breeds excitement. It usually happens because it is *quicker* and *easier* to build this way. *Largeness* is sometimes produced, but seldom *longevity*.

Innovation is prioritized over the anointing. Man-made ideas are implemented to achieve production. In our generation, there is no shortage of creative ways to produce revival. As King David trying to bring the Ark of the Covenant back to Israel, we have produced thousands of "new carts" in our attempts to bring back the glory. They come disguised in many forms, from church growth seminars to the most innovative and technologically brilliant schemes imaginable. (And many of them with good motive, I might add.) E.M. Bounds said it well, "We are constantly on a stretch, if not a strain, to devise new methods, new plans, new organizations to advance the Church and secure enlargement and efficiency for the gospel."[2]

I sometimes hear talk of mighty meetings, but find only hype and sensationalism when I arrive. I hear words like "impact" and "change", but see very little of it after the meetings. I heard of one well-known evangelistic team's great crusade a few years back where more than 2,000 young people were supposedly won to Christ in a single week. A few months later I checked the lasting results in the area and could find only one convert in a local church. Revival? I don't think so.

This weakness results in what I term "placebo Christianity." The outside looks good, but the inside lacks substance. It looks alive, but is dead. Perhaps most alarming is that it standardizes mediocrity. The Church of America now has this disease.

The Samson Effect

An overemphasis on power, miracles and emotional stirrings always leads to sensationalism and, ultimately, a *decrease* in power. Like the church at Sardis, the life and anointing of the Holy Spirit die while the reputation of the church lives on. As with Samson, this can take place without us even being aware of it. "'I will go out as at other times and shake myself free.' But he did not know that the Lord had departed from him" (Judg. 16:20).

This pattern inevitably leads to cynicism on the part of the world and disillusionment in the Church. I have watched several churches and ministries built this way. Excitement prevailed, Christians transferred and these works became the latest "fastest-growing, cutting-edge, overnight sensation." The magazines came, articles were written, television shows were produced and money was made. Many of them are now dead or mortally wounded. Others still have a name that they're alive, but are basically dead. Heaven weeps while we go do it somewhere else, creating another overnight sensation, playing our kingdom success games.

And what is the fruit? Our cities and nation are no different—no, that's not really true. They are much worse! Generation X still waits for something real. Christians grow more disillusioned, the world more cynical.

I will know this perversion of truth is broken off the Church in America when church janitors, longtime Sunday School teachers, no-name intercessors, nursery workers, and any number of other good and faithful servants make the cover of our magazines and are interviewed on our television programs—when we begin to judge the way heaven judges, when we glorify what God glorifies! When I see loyalty lauded over transiency, faithfulness over flashiness, consistency over charisma and substance over sensation, I'll know things are changing. "Too strong, Dutch" you say? Not as strong as the Bible. Jesus said our lukewarmness makes Him want to throw up (see Rev. 3:16).

Genuine Greatness

I don't think we understand greatness at all. Most of us will be totally confused at the awards ceremony in heaven. I can assure you of this: It won't look like ours. I have some truly great people in my fellowship. You won't hear of most of them until we get to heaven. They're not "gifted" enough. They're simply great moms and dads, great workers, great servants.

My grandfather, Bill Henkel, died recently. He was almost 90. He didn't leave me a penny. It wasn't there to leave. He lived in a small house in a small town. He never preached a sermon, but his life continues to speak. So does his seed. Known for his integrity, my grandfather's handshake and his word were enough for anyone who knew him, *including his bank.* My brother once saw him get a loan at the bank without even a signature! He was truly humble. When he was saved, he crawled to the altar. He was in church every Sunday, most Wednesdays, and served in various capacities. He tithed and gave to many needy people, though he had to work two and sometimes three jobs to survive. He only had an elementary education. His children love God; his grandchildren preach the gospel.

He was a great man! Heaven celebrated his arrival. I wept and rejoiced at the legacy he left me, worth far more than money.

Understanding sensation and hype better than we in the Church do, the world is crying out for some substance from us "God-people." We will never reach them using their own methods. A capitalistic, "may the best man win" world is waiting to see some true love—giving, sacrificial, preferring one another, unconditional agape.

A proud, be-the-best, claw-your-way-to-the-top generation would be defenseless to genuine humility and servanthood.

A people who created the hydrogen bomb and went to the moon, but can't control its own flesh or keep a family together, would be immeasurably impacted by a display of true inner strength.

A race so desperate for the supernatural that it will embrace almost any new weird religion or psychic, would bow the knee if the true and living God were allowed to answer by fire, working some genuine miracles in their midst.

Let's shake off the shackles of perverted theology and its dead religion! Let's raise the standard back to the biblical level. Let's not be merely human, let's be Christ-ians—little Christs.

Let's insist on the real thing. Let's allow the river to flow.

God and the world are waiting.

Notes
1. Edward K. Rowell, *Fresh Illustrations for Preaching and Teaching* (Grand Rapids: Baker Books, 1997), p. 71.
2. E.M. Bounds, *Power Through Prayer* (Grand Rapids: Baker Book House, 1977), p. 5.

CHAPTER EIGHT

Pouring a Slab and Throwing a Party

Having discussed in our last chapter three weaknesses of the charismatic and Jesus movements, weaknesses which still exist in much of the Body of Christ, we now want to look at two more. Again, my purpose is not to criticize, but to help us to avoid repeating the mistakes of the past.

As the river of God continues to rise, we want to ensure that it flows unabated. We desire to obey Hebrews 12:1: "Lay aside every encumbrance, and the sin which so easily entangles us, and let us run with endurance the race that is set before us."

To assist us, our loving Father is bringing revelation, repentance and turning. He is disciplining us, not out of cruelty or a punishing motivation, but to bring an increase of "the peaceful fruit of righteousness" (Heb. 12:11). He is training us.

The word "trained" in this same verse is the Greek word *gumnazo*. We get the word gymnasium from it. God is taking us to the gym for some spiritual fitness exercise. He wants us to win the race. He's a great trainer and a loving Father. We can trust Him. We must remember this as we look at our weaknesses.

Rejoicing Without Reflecting,
Merriment Without Mourning

The fourth of these past and present weaknesses—*rejoicing without reflecting, merriment without mourning*—is illustrated in an interesting passage of Scripture, Ezra 3:10-13:

> Now when the builders had laid the foundation of the temple of the Lord, the priests stood in their apparel with trumpets, and the Levites, the sons of Asaph, with cymbals, to praise the Lord according to the directions of King David of Israel. And they sang, praising and giving thanks to the Lord, saying, "For He is good, for His lovingkindness is upon Israel forever."
>
> And all the people *shouted with a great shout* when they praised the Lord because the foundation of the house of the Lord was laid. Yet many of the priests and Levites and heads of fathers' households, the old men who had seen the first temple, *wept with a loud voice* when the foundation of this house was laid before their eyes, while many shouted aloud for joy; so that the people could not distinguish the sound of the shout of joy from the sound of the weeping of the people, for the people shouted with a loud shout, and the sound was heard far away (italics mine).

As the book of Ezra opens, Cyrus, king of Persia, has allowed a remnant of Israelites to return to Jerusalem for the purpose of rebuilding the Temple. Seventy years prior, Israel, because of their apostasy, had been taken into captivity by Nebuchadnezzar, king of Babylon. They came under the rule of Cyrus when he conquered Babylon. God then moved the heart of Cyrus, an idolatrous king, to allow them to return to Jerusalem, and even stirred his spirit to help them raise the needed funds (see Ezra 1:1-4).

(Wicked, ungodly politicians are not the problem in America, contrary to what most of the Church believes. God is capable of dealing with them—one way or another. When He doesn't, we need to ask why.)

A remnant of Israelites had returned under the leadership of Zerubbabel, and work on the Temple had begun. The celebration we read of was after they had laid the foundation.

Notice the contrasts in this passage. Some were rejoicing so loudly it was heard far away. Others, such as the old men who had seen the first Temple, were weeping with a loud voice. It must have been quite an event to witness.

We are not told why the older ones were weeping. Perhaps because the restoration was beginning, or maybe they were remembering the pain of the captivity with its tragic loss. They could have been reflecting on the former glory of the Temple and thinking how far away they were from its full restoration. They might have even been lamenting the apostasy that created its destruction. We are never told the reason. I think a good guess would be all of the above. One thing is certain: They had a different outlook. While many were laughing, these men were crying.

The problem with this fourth weakness has to do with our *perspective*, our need for a balanced approach to life and ministry. We need a proper mix of tears and laughter, fun and work, joy and mourning.

Fraiser of Lisuland in northern Burma translated the Scriptures into the Lisu language and then left a young fellow with the task of teaching the people to read.

When he returned six months later, he found three students and the teacher seated around a table, with the Scriptures opened in front of the teacher. When the students each read, they left the Bible where it was. The man on the left read it sideways, the man on the right read it sideways but from the other side, and the man across from the teacher read it upside down. Since they always occupied the same chairs, that's how each had learned to read, and that's how each thought the language was written.

We, too, can be like that. When we see something from only one perspective, we may think it's the only perspective. Sometimes it's good to change seats to assume a different perspective on the same truth.[1]

Too little rejoicing makes us dull and religious. It results in oppression, legalism, the destruction of zeal and vision and the sapping of strength and vigor. (The joy of the Lord is our strength. See Neh. 8:10.) It also makes our message terribly unappealing. You've probably heard of the sour-faced Christian who approached the wino with the invitation to go to church with him. Taking a long look at him, the wino replied, "No, thanks. I have problems enough of my own."

Nothing in this passage suggests that the rejoicing of the people was improper. In fact, the opposite seems true—it was a good thing. And it is for us as well. When God gave me the vision of His river, the joy of the Lord Himself amazed me.

Premature Celebration
On the other hand, too much rejoicing and we tend to lose sight of the essentials, such as our cause and the condition of the world. This is precisely what happened to these Israelites. They poured a slab and threw a party. Shortly thereafter, however, they abandoned the rebuilding process for 16 years. The love of pleasure and ease can rob us of our willingness to work, sacrifice and "endure hardship as a good soldier" (2 Tim. 2:3, *NKJV*).

The Israelites abandoned their work because of fear, discouragement, political pressure (see Ezra 4:4,5) and selfishness (see Hag. 1,2). Other people in the area, who didn't want the Temple rebuilt, hired political lobbyists to work against them, spreading rumors of rebellion to the king, and eventually the intimidation accomplished its goal. By the time the mortar of the foundation set up, fear and discouragement set in.

They used the excuse that it wasn't yet God's *opportune time* (Hebrew word *eth*—Hag. 1:2) for the Temple to be restored. After all, they reasoned, there wouldn't be all this opposition if it really was God's opportune time. So the building of the Temple stopped for 16 years—all they had was a party slab. Then they conveniently decided it *was* time for them to build their own homes and businesses. To turn them to repentance, God raised up the prophet Haggai to warn them of their deception.

"Consider your ways!" he cried.

> "Is it time for you yourselves to dwell in your paneled houses while this house lies desolate?" Now therefore, thus says the Lord of hosts, "Consider your ways! You have sown much, but harvest little; you eat, but there is not enough to be satisfied; you drink, but there is not enough to become drunk; you put on clothing, but no one is warm enough; and he who earns, earns wages to put into a purse with holes" (Hag. 1:4-6).

This description of the lack of fruitfulness in Israel could well describe America, including the Church of America. We produce more than any other nation, but it isn't enough—our greed is insatiable. Despite our wealth, our debt is overwhelming. The land of the free is now the home of the bound.

And what of the Church? Much home-building has gone on, but it hasn't been His. A Church, whose heritage is to be the lender, probably spends more annually in interest to banks than it does to evangelize the world. We have done less with more than possibly any generation of believers in Church history. Our greatest growth of late has been that of our debt and apathy. And as with the Israelites of Ezra's time, discouragement and fear are now prevalent for many of the same reasons: our own failures and seeming lack of fruitfulness, the attack and ridicule of the world, and the overall state of affairs in the earth.

"Consider your ways!" is a word to us today. It is time to stop doing our own thing, building our own kingdoms and seeking our own gain. It is time to build the Lord's house! It IS the opportune time! He who changes the times and seasons is doing it again (see Dan. 2:21). My prayer is that the age of apathy towards God's agenda comes to a screeching halt—that God pulls the legs out from under our easy chairs.

In Haggai's day, the message had its desired effect. Biblical repentance occurred—revelation, repentance (a new understanding) and turning God's way. Work on the Temple resumed and so

—

We are not at the mercy of politicians
and lobbyists. They can't stop the river
—as long as we obey the Lord.

——

did God's favor and blessing. He eliminated the political pressure, removed the influence of the lobbyists and brought restoration.

Can He do this today? Absolutely! When we respond to Him, as these Israelites did, He will once again bless our labors as He did theirs, and we will see there is no longer any basis for our discouragement and fears. We are not at the mercy of the politicians and evil lobbyists in our nation's capital. They can't stop the restoration or the river, as long as we obey the Lord. God never predicated revival on what they do. He can *move* the heart of the king (politicians) or *remove* him. Revival is determined by us. "If *my* people, which are called by my name, shall humble themselves, and pray, and seek my face, and turn from their wicked ways; then will I hear from heaven, and will forgive their sin, and will heal their land" (2 Chron. 7:14, *KJV*, italics mine).

As the comic strip "Pogo" said, "We have met the enemy, and he is us."

Blessed Are Those Who Mourn
Sometimes we, as these Israelites, allow our partying to be premature. It is so much easier and fun to party than to work. And celebrating is certainly more fulfilling than mourning.

The pain on the earth—hunger, war, poverty, abuse, rape, the spiritually lost—is often too depressing to think about. Sometimes I want to silence the Mother Teresas of the world. I want to rejoice so loudly that I can't hear their tears. They rain on my spiritual parade.

Somehow, we must learn to rejoice over our successes and the good things of life without being blinded or intoxicated by them. Our ostrich eyes are caked with mud and sand. We must be able to enjoy the goodness of our God and the joy of our salvation without it anesthetizing us to the pain around us and the fact that billions still haven't heard the good news. Somehow, we must marry the two. "Jesus...for the *joy* set before Him *endured* the cross, despising the *shame*" (Heb. 12:2, italics mine).

We must allow ourselves to be touched by the pain around us. Our Father does. He'll watch every one of the 4,000 abortions in America today. With the broken heart of a loving Creator, He'll reread the plans He had written for them in His book of destinies (see Ps. 139:16). He'll weep over the millions of fatherless children searching for identity. His heart will break as the stomachs of the hungry gnaw. He is looking for someone to share His pain. Are we too busy partying?

Merriment without mourning created a lot of trouble in the charismatic movement. We didn't know how to mourn. We lost the ability to weep. I have been rebuked by pastors for trying to awaken people to the pain and need of humanity. They didn't like sending their members home unhappy, spoiling their Sunday dinners. They might have left and gone to another fellowship where they could hear what they wanted and party on.

As the crowd listened to the aforementioned testimony of Holy Hubert, I recall how we clapped about what he wept to get. It seemed a bit unfair to me. I couldn't help but reflect on how easy it was for us—and how costly for him.

I remember, in my early days participating in the movement, disliking and turning off to some with genuine burdens from the Lord. I wanted to laugh, dance, rejoice and confess the blessings of the Lord, not be knocked off my "high" by someone with a burden. Heaven must have wept as we laughed.

The Holy Spirit tried to get our attention through some fathers who had enough wisdom to see what we couldn't. One of them was a man named Charles Duncombe. "Brother D," as so many called him, was older—a wealth of wisdom, very sensitive

141

to the Holy Spirit—and considered a true father in the Lord by many. Also being a great and eloquent speaker, he was in much demand.

In the early '80s, however, he brought a warning to the charismatic movement. Seeing the shallowness and deception of much that was happening, especially the inward focus and the "bless me" mind-set which had set in, he tried his best to sound the alarm.

Was he listened to? Far from it—it was party time! He was ostracized by the Body of Christ. By the time he died, Brother D couldn't get a meeting. People didn't want to hear the warning. Most of us were too blinded by our celebrations to see the reality of the situation.

He wrote a powerful booklet entitled *Blessed Are Those Who Mourn*, trying once again to awaken us. He could find no one who would even consider publishing it. It was too confrontive, offensive, controversial, alarming, non-charismatic. It wouldn't have sold well, and after all, prosperity *was* the bottom line. So they published more books on how to prosper and succeed—Christian *Think and Grow Rich* stuff.

He gave the manuscript to me shortly before he died, saying, "You can have it; no one else wants it." To this day it sits on my bookcase, screaming its indictment against us. We're listening now—the party's over.

On the last page of the booklet, Brother Duncombe said, "I mourn because the great charismatic move of the last few decades is not headed for revival."

The verdict is in. We produced growth, not disciples. We prospered greatly, and focused it all inward. Our liberty in the spirit became license. Our new-found independence from traditions and dead forms turned to independent spirits.

And God turned away.

The movement died, a season of correction came and now, in His sovereign wisdom and great mercy, God is bringing forth another season of restoration. Will it become revival in America as it has in other parts of the world? It can and I pray it will. If it is going to happen, however, we're going to need a little more mourning, sowing the precious tear seeds spoken of in Psalm 126. *Then* we can rejoice, bringing in the sheaves of harvest.

Elishas Without Elijahs

The last of the five pitfalls that short-circuited these move-ments—*Elishas Without Elijahs*, sons without fathers, ministers without mentors—speaks of the need we all have for spiritual fathers in our lives.

Let me say from the beginning, when I speak of spiritual fathers and sons, I am not referring to gender. I am speaking of function. Women certainly can and do fulfill the biblical criteria for sonship and fathering, in the same way we men are a part of the Bride of Christ. We are speaking of the relational aspect and the need it fulfills, not the particular gender.

There came a point in my walk when I recognized my great need and found myself asking, almost in a murmuring way, "Where have all the fathers gone?" Sometime later I realized what had happened to many of them—they were run over and trampled by us young zealots.

They didn't have the speed, muscle and fire that we Ahimaazes and Asahels had (see the previous chapter) and rather than honoring their experience and wisdom, allowing them to father us, we pulled an Absalom. We cast them aside, took their pulpits and/or members and "showed them how to do it."

We were *teknons* (teenagers) showing the *paters* (fathers) how to run (the five stages of maturity discussed in chapter 4). And run we did—into buildings, trees, pits and anything else in our way. We never did find the finish line, but we arrived there first! God is still cleaning up the mess.

I am not a church historian, but I cannot imagine a movement in church history that placed so many novices in ministry posi-tions. Why did it happen? Because of our emphasis on speed, size and gifting. A few years down the road, with our churches struggling, our members disillusioned and the world laughing, we began to cry out for fathers.

Some of them are cautiously beginning to rise from the rubble of rejection and wonder if there really is a place for them after all. Others who have experienced the frustration of being fatherless (though perhaps self-inflicted) have allowed the Lord to develop them and bring them into fatherhood. Thank God He is raising up spiritual fathers.

I spoke to the spiritual father of a well-known minister a few years back, sharing concerns I saw in this minister's life and ministry. The father agreed.

"Why don't you do something?" I asked.

"He no longer listens to me," the father answered with obvious concern. "He's too big...too popular...too important."

It should come as no surprise that this young man has since been publicly exposed for his lack of integrity in ministry.

Never outgrow your need for Dad! What happens when we do? What did our independence produce in the charismatic movement?

- Leaders who produce action without accountability.
- *Works*-oriented ministries that don't know the *ways* of God.
- Lording leaders who haven't learned to lead by serving.
- The prostituting of gifts for gain.
- Leaders who know how to birth children, but not how to train and nurture sons and daughters.

The Fruits of Spiritual Fatherhood
If we allow them to, what will spiritual fathers teach and produce in us?

- Seeing the subtleties of pride and selfish ambition, they teach us humility.
- Recognizing the danger of isolation and one-person shows, they teach us dependence—our need for one another.
- Understanding the seasons of the Spirit, they teach us patience—the ability to wait.

144

- Knowing you can't build on miracles, sensation and the works of God, they teach us the ways of God and the principles of His Word.
- Knowing the strength and subtlety of sin, they demonstrate the need for and provide accountability.
- Helping us become fathers, they prevent the next generation from being spiritually illegitimate.
- They remove the curse from the land (see Mal. 4:6).
- They prevent haste without heart, speed without seasoned skill, sensationalism without substance and rejoicing without reflecting, thereby preserving the flow of the river.

It is no accident the Scriptures say the young men see *visions*, the old men dream *dreams* (see Joel 2:28). One possible interpretation of this is that vision points ahead, while literal dreams are born of things we have seen or experienced in our past. One causes us to run *aggressively* (vision), the other with *perspective* (dreams). When the foundation for the Temple was poured, the visionaries partied, the dreamers wept. Both are essential!

The Cleansing Power of the River

In order to correct these and other weaknesses in the Church, God has begun a work of cleansing: revelation, repentance and turning. The depth of the river diminished to a trickle as He exposed sin, flesh, carnality, wrong motives and unscriptural ways. He loves us too much to allow our weaknesses to rob us of our destinies; He loves the lost too much to allow our weaknesses to rob them of His river. So the correction continues.

This cleansing by the Lord was often typified in Scripture by the wilderness east of the Jordan River. Israel's 40 years of wandering and Christ's 40 days of testing are examples. Isaiah 40:3,4 speaks of it and says the cleansing that takes place there prepares the way for God to move again. Isaiah 35:8 calls this way a "Highway of Holiness."

Three parallel pairs in the Scriptures illustrate this pattern:

Moses and Joshua, Elijah and Elisha, John the Baptist and Jesus. The first in each pairing had a wilderness ministry. They had preparatory, cleansing ministries which paved the way for new seasons of blessing and greater anointings of the Holy Spirit in the Promised Land...a new flow of the river, if you please, pictured by the second in each group.

Moses led the children of Israel in the wilderness. Because of his and Israel's sin, they could not go into the Promised Land. The sin was purged from them *in the wilderness*, after which Joshua could take God's people into the land of blessing, victory and abundance. For us, Moses pictures repentance; Joshua symbolizes revival, a deep flow of the river.

Elijah (a type of John the Baptist) had a wilderness, cleansing ministry. He was the fiery prophet who challenged the wicked Jezebel, Ahab and the prophets of Baal. He was also instrumental in bringing about God's judgment of drought. Elijah called the nation to repentance (see 1 Kings 18).

Elijah "was of the settlers of Gilead" (1 Kings 17:1), which is east of the Jordan (the wilderness). He was hidden and cared for by God at "the brook Cherith, which is east of the Jordan" (v. 3). He was also provided for by a widow in Zarephath, which means "refinement" and was also east of the Jordan.

As a final depiction of his preparatory, cleansing ministry, Elijah was taken away by a whirlwind to heaven from the wilderness (east) side of the Jordan. The location was planned by God. "The Lord has sent me to the Jordan," Elijah said to Elisha in 2 Kings 2:6. He didn't stop at the Jordan, however, but crossed *into the wilderness* where he was taken. Elisha then received the greater anointing and went back into the Promised Land, just as Joshua had. His ministry, too, signals revival, a new outpouring of the Holy Spirit, the river.

The Bulldozer Anointing

John the Baptist had perhaps the best-known wilderness ministry. In John 1:23 he declared, "I am a voice of one crying in the wilderness, 'Make straight the way of the Lord.'" Three times it was said of him he ministered "beyond the Jordan" (see John 1:28; 3:26; 10:40).

John the Baptist paved the way for the new and greater anointing. "Clear the way" is the action foretold of him in Isaiah 40:3. "Then the glory of the Lord will be revealed," verse five continues. The way must be prepared for God's glory—renewal,

---

If God did not do a work of cleansing
in the Church before sending His glory,
His presence would devastate us.

---

restoration, revival, awakenings, the river. Isaiah said the valleys, mountains, rough ground and rugged terrain must all be cleared into a highway.

I term this the "bulldozer anointing." When a road is being built it gets very messy before it gets nice. Mud, holes, metal rods, heavy equipment, sloppy concrete, roadblocks and detours are part of the process of building a road. We tolerate it, however, because we envision a nice, new, smooth road to travel.

God begins the passage in Isaiah 40 by saying, "Comfort, O comfort My people" (v. 1). He then describes and prophesies the bulldozer anointing of John the Baptist. John's message went something like, "Repent, you bunch of snakes" (see Matt. 3:7,8).

Comfort?

Yes, comfort. The comfort isn't in the process—the clearing, bulldozing and repenting. The comfort is the end result. A highway is prepared for God. A channel for the river. The glory can come. The ministry of Jesus can flow.

God is too just and kind to bless us in our sin. And His glory is too strong, consuming sin and idols. If He did not do a work of cleansing before sending it, His glory would devastate us.

John the Baptist came with the message of repentance. That *is* the message of the wilderness, and it results in the ability to turn His way. Foretelling the ministry of John, an angel said:

"And he will *turn* back many of the sons of Israel to the Lord their God. And it is he who will go as a forerunner before Him in the spirit and power of Elijah, to *turn* the hearts of the fathers back to the children, and the disobedient to the attitude of the righteous; so as to *make ready* a people prepared for the Lord" (Luke 1:16,17, italics mine).

Christ could then come with the greater anointing, releasing the river of God, bringing deliverance and God's favor and glory. Not in the wilderness, but in the Promised Land of inheritance.

America, Strengthen the Things That Remain

The Church has been in the wilderness. In the 1980s God began this work of cleansing in the Church. Many people called it a shaking, and a shaking it was (see Heb. 12:25-29; Hag. 2:6,7). God began a ruthless work of exposing sin, impure motives and carnal ways in the American Church. Some blamed it on the devil, but it was God.

I don't think He is finished. Too much sin, compromise, apathy and lukewarmness linger in us. There has been change, but not enough. Most of our optimism in this land is nothing more than denial.

We are like the boy who was trying out for a part in the school play. He had his heart set on being in it, and his mother was concerned he would not be chosen. On the day the parts were announced, the boy rushed up to his mother, eyes shining with pride and excitement. "Guess what, Mom," he shouted. "I've been chosen to clap and cheer."[2]

That's good denial; ours isn't. We seem to think we are the only empire that can never become a has-been. America continues to lose ground to sin and perversion. Whether true or not, in a recent survey 70 percent of Americans essentially said it made no difference to them if their president was an adulterer. As long as prosperity and a strong economy exist, they want him left alone. This is so alarming, some in the world even see this as indicating a frightening loss of moral bearings. A recent issue of our local paper carried an editorial titled, "If Times Are Good, That's All That Matters."[3] We are a nation on a collision course with judgment. And for the most part, believers are sleeping through it.

We are a religious nation, not a godly nation. Jesus denounced the Pharisees as "whitewashed tombs" (Matt. 23:27). We are much the same. We look good outwardly, but the stench of death is inside. We say, as the church at Laodicea, "I am rich...and have need of nothing" (Rev. 3:17).

To this the Lord says:

"You do not know that you are wretched and miserable and poor and blind and naked. I advise you to buy from Me gold refined by fire, that you may become rich, and white garments, that you may clothe yourself, and that the shame of your nakedness may not be revealed; and eye-salve to anoint your eyes, that you may see. Those whom I love, I reprove and discipline; be zealous therefore, and repent" (Rev. 3:17-19).

His admonition to Sardis is also appropriate. "Wake up, and strengthen the things that remain, which were about to die; for I have not found your deeds completed in the sight of My God" (Rev. 3:2).

It would be a dangerous deception to blame America's problems on the unsaved. We, the salt and light of God, have allowed much of our nation's decay through our prayerlessness and compromise. We have lowered the standard. And so the discipline of the Father continues.

In *Is It Real When It Doesn't Work?* Doug Murren and Barb Shurin recount:

Toward the end of the nineteenth century, Swedish chemist Alfred Nobel awoke one morning to read his own obituary in the local newspaper: "Alfred Nobel, the inventor of dynamite, who died yesterday, devised a way for more people to be killed in a war than ever before, and he died a very rich man."

Actually, it was Alfred's older brother who had died; a newspaper reporter had bungled the epitaph.

But the account had a profound effect on Nobel. He decided he wanted to be known for something other than developing the means to kill people efficiently and for amassing a fortune in the process. So he initiated the Nobel Prize, the award for scientists and writers who foster peace.

Nobel said, "Every man ought to have the chance to correct his epitaph in midstream and write a new one."[4]

God is giving us a chance to change our epitaph. If written now it would read, "Weighed in the balances and found wanting." It is not too late. There are signs of hope. The prayer movement, men's movement, unity, breakthroughs among youth, renewal—all these indicate things may be changing. Perhaps the most encouraging sign of all is that the Holy Spirit continues to cleanse and awaken.

Will this wilderness season bring the needed correction, or at least change it to the point that revival can come? Does turning back to God bring revival, or does revival bring the turning? Both. If enough people hear what God is saying, repent and turn to Him, God will bring the river of His Spirit to us in such a way that others are swept in. They will then be touched by the fire and cleansing of the Lord.

It is time we return to Him with all of our hearts, with fasting, weeping and mourning, rending our hearts and not our garments (see Joel 2:12,13). "Who knows whether He will not turn and relent, and leave a blessing behind Him" (v. 14).

Thank God, to correct our deficiencies He initiated another time of cleansing and the *process* of revival began. We have been through shakings. We've gone to the wilderness. We have visited Hebrews 12—Dad is showing us we're not fatherless and we are loved. The forerunning ministries of John the Baptist, Moses and

Elijah have been released. The Cross is being resurrected. (How's that for an oxymoron?)

Hallelujah! The *process* of repentance has begun the *process* of revival. The river can and will flow in increasingly deeper levels if we cooperate with the Holy Spirit.

We, the Church, can either stumble our way through this wilderness process and hope we eventually make it across the Jordan into our destined purpose, or with understanding we can follow the cloud as it leads us through the preparatory dealings of God, and get on with the business of moving into the Joshua, Elisha and Jesus ministries. The wilderness is NOT our destiny. Canaan—where we possess our inheritance, eat the fruit of our salvation and function in our God-ordained role as "the light of the world" (Matt. 5:14)—is our destiny!

No more denial! Don't stay on the sidelines clapping and cheering. You have a part to play. Let the river flow through you.

Notes

1. Craig Brian Larson, *Illustrations for Preaching and Teaching* (Grand Rapids: Baker Books, 1993), p. 179. Adapted.
2. Jack Canfield and Mark Victor Hansen, *A Third Serving of Chicken Soup for the Soul* (Deerfield Beach, FL: Health Communications, Inc., 1996), p. 239. Adapted.
3. Mike Barnicle, "Commentary," *The Gazette* (Colorado Springs), February 16, 1998, News section p. 5.
4. Larson, *Illustrations for Preaching and Teaching*, p. 123.

CHAPTER NINE

Epoch-Making Revival

We have said revival begins with the process of repentance. In order for the river to flow in and from us unabated, the obstacles must be removed from its path. We must be adjusted to God's way of thinking.

God's cleansing, however, is always to prepare us for greater fruitfulness.

- The pruning of the Father produces "more fruit" (John 15:2).
- The discipline of the Father causes a greater yield of "the peaceful fruit of righteousness" (Heb. 12:11).
- The breaking up of the fallow ground allows for the rain of righteousness (see Hos. 10:12).
- In Elijah's day the judgment of drought prepared the way for a season of "abundance of rain" (1 Kings 18:41, KJV). The drought symbolized a lack of God's blessing. The rain represents a release of the flow of His river.
- Jesus cleansed the Temple and followed the act by healing the blind and lame (see Matt. 21:12-14).
- Jacob had his thigh dislocated by the Lord, then was blessed with a new name (Israel) and nature (see Gen. 32:24-32).

The Scriptures are filled with such examples of cleansing preparing the way for blessing. Interestingly, several are associated with water—rivers, streams, rain.

Jacob's cleansing from his scheming, conniving nature came at the *stream* Jabbok, which means "pouring out." His possessions were poured out (sent ahead to appease Esau). His strength was poured out (the thigh symbolized strength). His nature and identity were poured out ("What is your *name?*"). God then *poured in* a new nature (Israel). He revealed Himself in a new way ("I have seen God face-to-face"). Then He was able to fulfill this man's destiny of blessing the world through his seed (Jesus).

Naaman was cleansed of physical leprosy and the spiritual leprosy of pride at the *river* Jordan (see 2 Kings 5:14).

Just after crossing the *Jordan River*, the Israelites were circumcised—cutting away the flesh before going in to possess the land (see Josh. 5:2-12). It was on this very day of circumcision that God said, "Today I have rolled away the reproach of Egypt from you" (v. 9).

As previously mentioned, Elijah's lack of *rain*—drought—prepared the way for cleansing and blessing, also symbolized by *rain*. Hosea's breaking produced a *rain* of righteousness.

The point of all this is the river (water) is consistently spoken of in Scripture in the context of cleansing. The cleansing then paves the way for the flow of the river to bless. Which brings us to the point of this chapter (and everyone said, "Hallelujah!"). If we respond to the current word of the Holy Spirit, allowing repentance to do its work, God will be able to complete the process of revival in America.

Unleashing the Waters

"Repent therefore and return, that your sins may be wiped away, in order that times of refreshing may come from the presence of the Lord" (Acts 3:19). We have previously discussed the phrase, "repent and return, that your sins may be wiped away." Now let's look at the effect of this: "*in order that* times of refreshing may come."

The phrase "times of refreshing" is loaded with meaning. "Times" is the word *kairos*, which, as we have already stated, means "opportune time." Settle it in your thinking once and for all: *Repentance and turning create opportune times for God to move.*

Wuest, a very literal translator of the New Testament, uses the following phrases to translate *kairos*: "epoch-making periods" (Acts 3:19); "strategic, significant period" (Acts 12:1); "strategic, epochal time" (Acts 19:23). Using these definitions, repentance and turning create epoch-making, strategic, significant periods for God to move by His Spirit. I don't know about you, but I'm ready for some "epoch-making" revival.

A Flood of Historic Proportions

I looked up the term "epoch-making" to make sure I understood it. It means "significant by virtue of ensuing historical developments."[1] Epoch means "a period of time characterized by momentous events or changes;"[2] and "a fixed point of time from which succeeding years are numbered."[3]

Now that I've put the dictionaries away and danced around my office for a while...that's what we're after! Momentous events and changes. A revival so great it is historical; one from which succeeding years are numbered. We speak of physical floods this way. The year is remembered, like the Johnstown Flood of 1889 or the Big Thompson Canyon (Colorado) Flood of 1976. The size is measured by how often one of that proportion comes—a 50-year flood or a 100-year flood. We want a flood of the river of God so great that people will speak of it the way they speak of physical floods:

- "Remember the Bangladesh Flood of 1987?"
- "This was a hundred-year flood."
- "What a devastating flood!"
- "It changed the very topography."

I want a revival of such monumental proportions it is epoch-making:

- "Remember the flood of God's Spirit in 1998?"
- "It was a 2,000-year flood. There's been nothing like it since Pentecost!"
- "What a devastating flood! It wiped out sin everywhere it went."
- "It changed the very face of America."

Epoch-making!

Breathe on Us, O God!

The word "refreshing" in Acts 3:19 is important. It is the word *anapsuxis*, from *ana* and *psucho*. Strong's says *ana* means "repetition, intensity or reversal."[4] Zodhiates agrees, adding the word "increase."[5]

Psucho is "to breathe, blow or refresh with cool air."[6]

Here are some definitions of the two words—*ana* and *psucho*—combined (*anapsucho* or *anapsuxis*):

- "to draw breath again"
- "to revive by fresh air"[7]
- "to cool or refresh with a breath"
- "to regain strength"
- "restoration"[8]

In this verse, Peter is saying if we respond to the Holy Spirit, it will create a *kairos* time for God to breathe or blow on us again; to revive us with a fresh breath; to restore us, giving us new strength to enable us to draw breath again.

I also like the concept of intensity. He wants to breathe on us again *intensely*. That would be epochal! Peter was apparently thinking back a few days to Pentecost, a real epoch-making event when the breath of God blew again intensely, once more filling humans with the life of God.

In Ezekiel 37:1-14, the dry bones represent spiritual death. First God caused them to come together, then put skin on them, "but there was no breath in them" (v. 8). The prophet was then told, "Prophesy to the breath...say to the breath, 'Come from the four winds, O breath, and breathe on these slain, that they may come to life'" (v. 9).

This is what happened in Genesis 2:7. God breathed into a lifeless body and brought His life to Adam. Peter thought back through history—Genesis, Ezekiel, Pentecost—and prophesied in Acts 3:19 that it could happen again if the people would obey the Holy Spirit.

It has happened since on numerous occasions:

- in the fourteenth century through John Wycliffe;
- in the fifteenth century through the Lollards movement;
- in the sixteenth century through Martin Luther and John Calvin;
- in the seventeenth century came the Puritan Revival;
- in the eighteenth century through the Wesleys, George Whitefield and others;
- in the nineteenth century a revival swept the United States, Scotland, Wales and England;
- and the twentieth century has seen the worldwide Pentecostal movement.

God isn't finished, however. He has another breath—another wind to blow on us. He wants to bring it with great intensity. The revivals in other parts of the world and the renewals of Toronto, Canada; England; and Pensacola, Florida, represent the beginnings of this great blowing of God's breath on the dry bones of the earth.

If we in the American church will respond to the current word of repentance, it will create the *kairos*—epoch-making, opportune time—for the Spirit of God to blow on us again. I believe I see it happening, but only in an infancy stage. We must continue the process.

157

Buy the Opportunity!

When the process of repentance and turning has fully created the *kairos* of *anapsuxis*, we must seize the moment. Twice the New Testament says to redeem the time (see Eph. 5:15-17; Col. 4:5, KJV). "To redeem" is *exagorazo*, meaning buy or purchase, and "time" is *kairos*—"buy the opportune, epoch-making time." Buy the opportunity!

Opportunities must be bought. They cost something—time, energy, abilities, money, our very lives. If we don't spend what is necessary and buy them, opportunities can also be lost.

When Apple Computer fell on difficult days a while back, Apple's young chairman, Steven Jobs, traveled from the Silicon Valley to New York City. His purpose was to convince Pepsico's John Sculley to move west and run his struggling company.

As the two men overlooked the Manhattan skyline from Sculley's penthouse office, the Pepsi executive started to decline Jobs's offer.

"Financially," Sculley said, "you'd have to give me a million-dollar salary, a million-dollar bonus, and a million-dollar severance."

Flabbergasted, Jobs gulped and agreed—if Sculley would move to California. But Sculley would commit only to being a consultant from New York. At that, Jobs issued a challenge to Sculley: "Do you want to spend the rest of your life selling sugared water, or do you want to change the world?"

In his autobiography *Odyssey*, Sculley admits Jobs's challenge "knocked the wind out of me." He said he'd become so caught up with his future at Pepsi, his pension, and whether his family could adapt to life in California that an opportunity to "change the world" nearly passed him by. Instead, he put his life in perspective and went to Apple.[9]

Let's not miss the opportunity to change our world! Let's buy it!

We Need Vision for the Harvest

Allow God to birth vision in you *now*—vision that will motivate you to faith and action. Vision is a life-changer, a rearranger. Its hunger can be insatiable, a motivating force *creating energy* and *energizing creativity*.

Vision moves us from mere mental assent to physical exertion. It separates the hearer from the doer, the convert from the disciple and mediocrity from excellence. *It is also what separates a ripe harvest from a reaped harvest* (see Matt. 9:37).

Men give up successful careers due to Holy Spirit-generated vision. Some have walked away from great fortune, others earthly fame as this awesome force of heaven moved into their lives. It messes things up, alters lifestyles, rocks the boat. It rarely goes with the flow—it creates it.

I remember hearing Wayne Myers, a well-known missionary from Mexico, speak in the first missions conference I attended. I was single at the time and still living at home, probably 22 or 23 years old. The first night he ended up with about a third of my bank account for the missions program of the hosting church. The second night he got the next third. You guessed it: The last night he got the rest. If there had been a fourth night I'd have been walking home—he'd have gotten my car!

There was no manipulation; he didn't *make* me give the money. No one took it from me. What happened? Some of the all-consuming, all-encompassing vision he has for reaching the world with the gospel was imparted to me—that impossible-to-explain, you-just-have-to-experience-it, Holy Ghost osmosis which sometimes happens. I've given to missions ever since.

I remember when vision came to me to reach out to those devastated by pain and suffering. It was 1976, February 10 to be exact. The country was Guatemala, the village was San Pedro, the setting was a food line. I was a server, dishing soup to hungry women and children who had lost everything the previous week in an earthquake that killed 30,000 people and left one million homeless. I vividly recall dishing the soup into cans, bottles, jars (whole or broken) and whatever else they could find to hold a lit-tle soup. I also remember looking at the last lady in line—a mother holding her 2- or 3-year-old child who likely hadn't eaten in days—and telling her there was "no more."

—

Oh, for eyes to see the potential harvest!
For insight to understand the times! God is
speaking clearly to those who are listening.

⌇

Things got all messed up in my life at that moment! I could no longer look the other way and pretend not to see the need of suffering humanity. I had looked into hungry eyes...hopeless eyes...haunting eyes. Plans had to be changed, spending habits altered. Priorities were rearranged. Vision had come to me. Things have never been quite the same since.

Oh, for eyes NOW to see the potential harvest. For ears to hear the word of the Lord. For insight to understand the times! God is speaking a clear word to those who are listening.

Can you feel the breeze of Pentecost picking up? No, it's not the rushing, mighty wind yet, but the breeze is beginning to blow. I feel it when I pray, worship and commune with Father. I feel it as I traverse this country trumpeting a wake-up call.

I hear the Father asking, "Can these bones live?" He is trying to awaken faith in us. If we will only hear and obey, Mr. Wind Himself is about to be unleashed.

I, as Elijah, hear the "sound of abundance of rain" (1 Kings 18:41, *KJV*). The sound isn't yet thunder—don't expect it to be that loud. It is a gentle rumbling in the distance. But it is ominous. It is the voice of the Lord.

If we can only hear that sound as Elijah did, the false prophets of Baal are in trouble! Look out Ahab and Jezebel! Our God will answer by fire (cleansing). The peoples will say, "The Lord, He is God" (turning), and the rains will come (the river of life).

Let the fire fall, Father. Finish your cleansing work—create a kairos season for the wind. Breathe on us again...intensely!

May we turn to you with all our hearts.

Let the rains come. We're dry and thirsty.

Let the river flow with great force. Bring a mighty flood! The Flood of 1998—and beyond!

In Jesus' Name, Amen.

Notes

1. *New Webster's Dictionary and Thesaurus of the English Language* (New York: Lexicon Publications, Inc., 1991 edition), p. 318.
2. Ibid., p. 318.
3. *The Consolidated Webster Encyclopedic Dictionary* (Chicago: Consolidated Book Publishers, 1954), p. 255.
4. James Strong, *The New Strong's Exhaustive Concordance of the Bible* (Nashville: Thomas Nelson Publishers, 1990), ref. no. 303.
5. Spiros Zodhiates, *Hebrew-Greek Key Study Bible—New American Standard* (Chattanooga: AMG Publishers, 1984; revised edition, 1990), p. 1804.
6. Spiros Zodhiates, *The Complete Word Study Dictionary* (Iowa Falls, Iowa: Word Bible Publishers, Inc., 1992), p. 1496.
7. Ethelbert Bullinger, *A Critical Lexicon and Concordance to the English and Greek New Testament* (Grand Rapids: Zondervan Publishing House, 1975), p. 631.
8. Geoffrey W. Bromiley, *Theological Dictionary of the New Testament, Abridged* (Grand Rapids: William B. Eerdmans Publishing Co., 1985), p. 1352.
9. Craig Brian Larson, *Illustrations for Preaching and Teaching* (Grand Rapids: Baker Books, 1993), p. 278.

CHAPTER TEN

Divine Disorder— The Paradox of Revival

Revival winds usually, if not always, come wrapped in the unexpected. I recall the charismatic winds of the '60s and '70s. It blew the minds and theologies of many of us when we saw Catholic priests and nuns being filled with the Spirit, dancing and lifting their hands to the Lord in worship. Many of us in classical Pentecostal groups had been taught that no one in the Catholic church was even saved. We told God in no uncertain terms He couldn't do this.

He didn't get the message.

I recall the first time I saw people dancing and leaping unto the Lord in a charismatic service. I had heard of "dancing in the Spirit" (as we called it) for years and had even seen it a few times. But to us Pentecostals, one only did this when the Holy Spirit "came upon" you and sort of "took control." You couldn't just be filled with joy and choose to do it. That would have been "of the flesh." *Any* dancing not done "in the Spirit" was *extremely* evil.

When I arrived at Christ For the Nations Institute as a Bible school student, I went early to the opening service to get a front-row seat. Another young man had the same idea, and as he plopped himself down beside me, he said, "We dancers like the front row and aisle seats."

We dancers? I thought. *What is this, some kind of a cult?* All of a sudden the first note sounded, the singing began, and bodies started flying everywhere!

My poor little traditional, legalistic Pentecostal mind went "Tilt!" I didn't know whether to run, crawl under the seat or cast out demons. I was so badly outnumbered, however, that I just closed my eyes and prayed. Every once in a while I would open one eye—just a little—to make sure no one was coming after me. I told the Lord if He would get me out of there safely, I wouldn't test Him again.

By the time the worship ended, however, I had sensed the presence of God in a mighty way. This was confusing, to say the least. I decided I might try just one more service. After all, God seemed to feel it was safe enough to show up. And, besides, I had already paid my tuition.

So I tried another...and another...and then another service. A couple of weeks later I was doing it! "We dancers like the front row and aisle seats," I found myself on occasion saying to poor, unsuspecting visitors.

It's funny how wrong we can be, and how right we can feel.

A Bulge Here, A Lump There...

Receiving the flow of the river is not optional if we want the fresh life of the Spirit. Ezekiel said, "Everything will live where the river goes" (Ezek. 47:9). But the "swamps and marshes will not become fresh [healed]; they will be left for salt" (v. 11, parenthetical word mine). Places where the river could not flow were left in their state of stagnation.

Why would some not receive the river? There are numerous reasons, some of which we'll look at in the next two chapters.

When the Bible talks about "old wineskins" in Matthew 9:17 and Luke 5:37-39, it is referring to individuals who are not able to receive the new wine of the Holy Spirit. We are all susceptible to this. Ralph Mahoney explains the symbolism well:

The new wine represents the new harvest of blessing and revival God wants to send. The wineskin is that which contains the new harvest....

The wineskin is made of sheep's skin. When it is originally prepared for use to contain wine, it is very flexible, pliable and elastic.

As the new wine begins fermenting, the wineskin stretches just like a balloon. As it swells, it gets into all kinds of unusual shapes. You get a bulge here and a lump there, and end up with an unusual, original shape. No two wineskins are the same.

Once the wine has been curing and aging for several years, the wineskin gets rigid. It becomes inflexible and stiff.

It is easy to see how this dry, brittle wineskin becomes a picture of a church or denomination that knew revival sometime in the past; however, its present condition is nothing like it was when God first sent the new wine of revival.[1]

All of us, as wineskins, harden into set ways of doing things—forms, rituals, liturgies, traditions. If God then brings something to our church service which violates our traditional sense of orthodoxy, we usually reject it. Our definition of orthodoxy defines what we will let Him do, instead of allowing what He does to define our orthodoxy. When this has happened, we have become "old wineskins" which cannot hold "new wine." We cannot flex and are therefore incapable of receiving the new.

A View from the Floor

Actually there is no biblical basis for the way we conduct our church services. There are numerous practices:

- The Catholics have a way.
- The Lutherans have a way.
- The Methodists have a way.

- The Baptists have a way.
- The charismatics have a way.

We all have our preferred methods, and everyone thinks theirs is the correct way!

What is really important when we come together? Doing what the Scriptures clearly teach—worship, the teaching of the Word, fellowship and prayer, for example. The order and method of doing them isn't sacred. Don't make doctrines out of methods, and don't equate doctrine with truth.

The same is true when the Holy Spirit chooses to minister to a person. Whether we touch them or anoint them with oil is not the main issue. Whether they stand or kneel, fall or remain on their feet is irrelevant. Whether they laugh or cry is unimportant. What matters is that they receive a touch from the Holy Spirit of God. Let Him do it! If having someone laugh in our services offends our sense of order or orthodoxy, maybe we should reconsider what we believe to be proper.

Most of us love laughing. To be able to sit and laugh for an hour is considered wonderful—we'll even pay someone to help us. But leave your joy and laughter in the darkened theater. Or keep it in your living room as you watch television. But don't bring it to church, for heaven's sake!

Acceptable positions are now defined by our orthodoxy and wineskin shapes also. It's okay for God to heal or minister comfort to someone—*as long as they are on their feet or seated in a pew.* But, PLEASE, not while they're lying on the floor! The following healing of a young lady in our fellowship took place on the floor. Here is her account of what happened:

> Intimacy has always been a struggle for me. I had tried counseling, ministry, prayer, but still found a major block in this area. At the end of a particular service, I went up for prayer and sensed the powerful presence of the Spirit of God. The person ministering simply took my hands and said, "Come with me into the presence of God." I was taken in the Spirit to another place.

God the Father was sitting on the throne talking to a group of angels. I was standing alone at the edge of the light coming from the throne, observing the scene. My heavenly Father stopped what He was doing, turned toward me, and with His head in His hands just looked at me. He didn't say anything. He didn't have to. He stopped what He was doing for me. His eyes were so incredibly loving and I had His attention. In that one moment of time, God healed wounds of rejection that were years old.

In almost every service since then, during worship I look up and can see His face looking at me with incredible love and acceptance.

Though this would violate the beliefs of many, the fruit in this young lady's life speaks for itself.

I'm afraid Jesus would have violated our orthodoxy and sense of order in many of His meetings. He allowed people to crawl to

---

The sad fact is that most believers
are more alive to the world than to the Lord.

Him, ask Him questions—He even allowed prostitutes to weep at His feet, bathing them with tears. *We could use a little Divine Disorder!*

Baptist evangelist Vance Havner once said, "The same church members who yell like Comanche Indians at a ball game on Saturday sit like wooden Indians in church on Sunday."[2]

Michael Brown says this "has nothing to do with being conservative. It has to do with the sad fact that most believers are more alive to the world than to the Lord."[3]

Don't mistake orthodoxy or your sense of order for truth, sound doctrine or correctness. Of course, it isn't wrong to become comfortable with certain methods or ways—unless they begin to control us.

How to Renew an Old Wineskin

The literal wineskins in Christ's day, as metaphors for our spiritual lives, needed to be renewed. The wineskins were soaked in water for several days, which for us symbolizes the Word of God (see Eph. 5:26). Then they were rubbed with oil, which of course symbolizes the Holy Spirit. If we will allow Him, the Lord will soften us with the Word and His Spirit until we can again receive new wine.

Interestingly enough, the word for "*new* wine" in this passage is different than the word for "*new* wineskin." The word for "new" in new wine is *neos* which means *numerically* new, but not *qualitatively* new. We receive new doses—outpourings of the Holy Spirit, but it is the same spiritual drink, the same wine. It may be packaged differently, He may pour it differently, but it is the same wine.

The *new* wineskin is derived from a different word for "new." The word is *kainos*, which means qualitatively new, different. The wine of the Spirit doesn't change, but we, the wineskins, must. We must allow the Holy Spirit to work newness into us, changing us from glory to glory. We cannot expect to stay the same, never changing size, shape or texture, and expect to be able to receive the new thing that God is doing. *Neos* wine must go into *kainos* skins.

We must be willing to change. We don't have the right to say to God, "Send revival, pour out Your Spirit, send the river, but do it *my way*. Conform to my shape and expectations." This is the mistake made by the religious people of Christ's day. They were, in fact, the reason for this teaching. Their preconceived ideas of the way Messiah was to come and what He was to look like kept them from recognizing and receiving Him. The One they had awaited for centuries didn't come packaged the way they felt He should, so they rejected Him. They saw the miracles, signs and wonders He performed, but it didn't matter. Their wineskins were just too rigid. They had put God in a box, and *their box was too small*.

Are we any different today? Sadly, most are not. We struggle with the new wine, usually because it isn't packaged in our brand of wineskins. It is no secret that those associated with former revivals frequently persecute the next one. In his book *Holy Fire*, Michael Brown makes this interesting observation:

> How sad that history often repeats itself. The early Methodists were persecuted and put out of churches by the hypocritical ministers of their day. Why? The Methodists broke with all rules and Church precedents by preaching the new birth on the streets and in the city squares. But one century later, it was the traditional Methodist ministers who persecuted the newly formed Salvation Army. Why? The Salvation Army preached the new birth on the streets and in the city squares![4]

Guy Chevreau, in *Catch the Fire*, shares the following quote from Spurgeon, who offers good advice:

> Observe how sovereign the operations of God are....He may in one district work a revival, and persons may be stricken down, and made to cry aloud, but in another place there may be crowds, and yet all may be still and quiet, as though no deep excitement existed at all....He *can* bless as He wills and He *will* bless as He wills. Let us not dictate to God. Many a blessing has been lost by Christians not believing it to be a blessing, because it did not come in the particular shape which they had conceived to be proper and right.[5]

As the river begins to rise in its depth, as God begins to move in our midst with a few supernatural signs—laughter, shaking, people falling—some reject it because it isn't what they have been used to. As Spurgeon admonished, let's not lose a blessing because it didn't come in our "shape."

What Do We Really Want?

Many of us want signs and wonders, but not wonders which make us wonder. We want controllable wonders. Logical wonders. Wonders which fit the shape of our skin. But I don't think it's a wonder if it doesn't make us wonder. I wonder what it is we really want.

We say we want revival, the river, even the supernatural. But if God chooses to make someone jerk under His power, it offends our minds and insults our intelligence. We want a supernatural God, but we don't want Him to do anything "unnatural." We want the supernatural naturally. We want wonders that don't violate our intellects. So we bring an omniscient, omnipotent God down to our natural level. When will we let Him be God to us? Do we really think we have Him totally figured out, that we fully understand Him? We all answer "No," but just let Him prove it, and we quickly show the shape and texture of our wineskins.

Initially George Whitefield was critical of the manifestations that took place in John Wesley's meetings. He had to change his opinion of what God would and wouldn't do. Wesley said:

> I had an opportunity to talk with [Whitefield] of those outward signs which had so often accompanied the inward work of God. I found his objections were chiefly founded on gross misrepresentations of matters of fact. But the next day he had an opportunity of informing himself better: for no sooner had he begun (in the application of his sermon) to invite all sinners to believe in Christ, than four persons sunk down close to him, almost in the same moment. One of them lay without either sense or motion; a second trembled exceedingly; the third had strong convulsions all over his body, but made no noise, unless by groans; the fourth, equally convulsed, called upon God, with strong cries and tears. From this time, I trust, we shall all suffer God to carry on His own work in the way that pleaseth Him.[6]

As stated earlier in the book, 1 Corinthians 2:14 says the things of the Spirit are foolish to natural man. The word foolish is *moria*, which means moronish. *The things of the Spirit are often going to be ridiculous to the natural mind.* The sooner we accept this, the better off we will be.

—

The river of God flows differently, requiring change.
Get ready to be changed or be bypassed.

—

We cannot expect a *supernatural* God to do things *naturally*. We should not expect the works of an all-wise God to always be explainable. A few word definitions will give weight to this.

Contrary to Popular Opinion

The Greek word for a "wonder", *teras*, means "startling, imposing, amazing."[7] It was used to describe what God did at Pentecost (see Acts 2:19).

The word "paradox", *paradoxa*, was used to describe the works of Jesus.

And they were all seized with astonishment and began glorifying God; and they were filled with fear, saying, "We have seen remarkable things today" (Luke 5:26).

"Remarkable things" is *paradoxa*. Literally the word means, "contrary to acceptable opinion"; something "which though true, seems false and self-contradictory."[8]

Zodhiates says *paradoxa* is "something beyond one's expectation, a miracle."[9]

By these definitions, Jesus was a paradox. He contradicted the experts, their traditions and opinions. John the Baptist was a paradox. Paul was a paradox. The odds are great that we, as most people, would have rejected all of them had we been around when they were on the earth—unless we could have changed our wineskins, that is.

The river of God is often *paradoxa*, contrary to acceptable opinion. It doesn't usually flow in denominational and/or traditional channels. Its very method of flowing is usually different and requires change. A flooded river creates new channels and courses; so will the river of God. Get ready to be changed or be bypassed. There will always be some who speak against it. Arthur Wallis wrote, "If we find a revival that is not spoken against, we had better look again to ensure that it is a revival."[10]

Peter almost opposed a move of God. God brought a *paradoxa* to him in Acts 10. Three times He showed him a vision of unclean food and told him to eat it. Everything about this violated his past training and sense of right and wrong. It was contrary to his accepted opinion.

Peter kept calling "unclean" what God was calling "clean." Don't forget that this referred to God pouring out His Spirit on the Gentiles (see Acts 10:28). Be careful you don't label a move of the Holy Spirit as "unclean." When God is doing something we don't understand or can't explain, perhaps even paradoxical, let's be humble enough to *plead* ignorance instead of *demonstrating* it. I've done the latter plenty of times. Just when I think I have God all figured out, He shows up on a donkey and spits in a man's eyes.

At least four reasons explain why people reject a new flow of the river of God when it comes accompanied by unusual manifestations.

1.   A Logical, Reasoning Motivation
Some people are so left-brained, or intellectually motivated, they have great difficulty accepting anything supernatural. If they can't understand or explain something, they simply reject it.

2.   A Fear of Losing Control
This affects many leaders who feel a legitimate responsibility to conduct meetings with order and safety. It isn't always easy to

know the difference between governing—which is good—and controlling. This problem also affects many people not in leadership. To be overcome with a power greater than themselves is a frightening thought. Unfortunately, this brings God to a human level and essentially says to Him, "Do what You want, as long as You leave me in control."

3.   Preconceived Ideas and Methods

We have already discussed this tendency somewhat. Our current paradigms control, or at the very least, influence all of us much more than we realize. This is what creates the old wineskin problem. When revival comes and rocks our boats, sometimes we anchor ourselves to the familiar. The results are often spiritual stagnation and, according to Christ, no new wine.

4.   Extremes

This will be discussed in the next chapter. It has to do with the worn-out cliché of throwing the baby out with the bath water, which is simply overreacting to extremes. We know the cliché well, yet many good things do go down the drain.

We must guard against these and other tendencies when we deal with the things of God. He is bigger than our theology, paradigms, minds, orthodoxy, fears and even the mistakes of others.

Allow Him to be God. He is and will be, whether we allow it or not, but not necessarily in our wineskins. Don't make Him bypass you with the new wine. Adapt your skin to accommodate His flow. Let the river come anyway He wants. Let Him even make you wonder—it's wonderful!

173

Notes

1. Ralph Mahoney, *Is a New Wave of Revival Coming?* (Burbank: World Missionary Assistance Plan, 1982), pp. 71, 72.

2. Michael L. Brown, *From Holy Laughter to Holy Fire* (Shippensburg, PA: Destiny Image Publishers, Inc., 1996), p. 122.

3. Ibid.

4. Ibid., p. 63.

5. Guy Chevreau, *Catch the Fire* (Toronto: HarperCollins Publishers, Ltd., 1994), p. 146.

6. Brown, *From Holy Laughter to Holy Fire*, p. 124.

7. Spiros Zodhiates, *Hebrew-Greek Key Study Bible—New American Standard* (Chattanooga: AMG Publishers, 1984; revised edition, 1990), p. 1881.

8. *New Webster's Dictionary and Thesaurus of the English Language* (New York: Lexicon Publications, Inc., 1991 edition), p. 727.

9. Zodhiates, *Hebrew-Greek Key Study Bible—New American Standard*, p. 1863.

10. Brown, *From Holy Laughter to Holy Fire*, p. 72.

CHAPTER ELEVEN

Are We as Balanced as We Think?

While I'm offending some of your concepts of what is and is not proper—what God will and won't do—have you ever *smelled* the presence of God?

Hey, if we can swim with Jesus and fly around the world with Him without an airplane, we might as well smell Him. It happened in the same series of meetings as the vision I spoke of in chapter 1.

Late one night—most people had left the meeting—about 20 of us remained in the church, basking in the presence of the Lord. Then it happened. We all began to notice this wonderful fragrance. It smelled like flowers, but there were none in the room.

The fragrance came and went for about an hour, moving from one part of the room to another. The Rose of Sharon, the Lily of the Valley, was manifesting His presence. It was incredible!

Perhaps more amazing was the story we heard later. One of the men of our fellowship had been prayed for earlier during the service and had fallen under the power of the Holy Spirit. He fell forward instead of backward.

He lay on his face for awhile, intermittently laughing and

crying. After a period of time, he began to crawl around the floor with his nose to the ground, eyes still closed. It was actually quite humorous at times. (This violated my sense of orthodoxy, by the way. My wineskin did some serious stretching that night!)

Later, when he became "normal" again, he told us the story. When he fell forward, he was immediately seeing a vision. He fell into a field of flowers. While we were watching him crawl around, nose to the floor, he was smelling the flowers in his vision.

In his vision he followed the field of flowers down to a stream. He sat down by this stream and began to look at pictures—pictures from his past. As he sat there looking at them, some of which represented painful experiences and sinful events, the Lord walked up to him.

"What are you looking at?" Jesus asked him.

"Oh, just some pictures of my life," the man answered.

"Can I see them?" asked the Lord.

The brother was a little embarrassed and responded, "Well, you don't really want to see these pictures, Lord. They're not very nice."

"Yes, I do. Let Me see them."

Reluctantly he handed one to the Lord. Jesus took it and began to fold it. *What is He doing?* wondered the brother. The Lord folded it into a boat, sat it on the stream and watched it float away.

"Can I have another?" He asked. Again He folded it and sent it away. This He did until they were gone.

What happened to this brother? Tremendous healing of painful memories from his past...carried away by the river of God. The weeping we had observed resulted from this healing taking place. The flowers we later smelled were those in this brother's vision.

I can hear some of you saying, "Pretty radical stuff, Sheets."

Yeah, I agree. Great, isn't it? *Please, Lord, come again with Your radical love and heal someone else. Let us smell Your presence again.*

"But why did He do it this way, Dutch?"

WHO CARES? I certainly don't know why and don't care. He is God and can do it anyway He wants. Extreme, isn't it?

Seasons of Imbalanced Emphasis

One of the reasons we reject revival is that, in a fresh, new move of His Spirit, God typically comes in extremes. Extreme manifestations, conviction, miracles, *even truth*. In fact, the Holy Spirit restores most truths to the Church with extreme emphasis. While He never comes with imbalanced truth or doctrine, He *will* restore truths with an imbalanced *emphasis*.

Before my critics organize a book burning, let me say I am *not* implying that doctrine or truth cannot or should not be balanced. Nor am I suggesting that God brings extremes or imbalances in the truths themselves. I am simply stating that He will bring an imbalanced *emphasis* for a season. For example, while it would never be proper to teach submission in a way that legitimizes control (imbalanced truth), it would not be wrong to heavily emphasize submission for a season (imbalanced emphasis). Likewise, it is legitimate to emphasize faith; it is illegitimate to say that if one has enough faith, he or she will never suffer.

Probably every revival or period of restoration in Church history has emphasized certain kingdom truths in a way that would typically represent an *over*emphasis. There's nothing improper about this. It is no different than a church, for example, having a season where missions is emphasized above everything else. This period of overemphasizing serves to establish missions in the life of the fellowship, at which time the emphasis in this area can then become "balanced."

I recently did a 12-week teaching in our fellowship on purpose and destiny. It accomplished what I desired and now I simply refer to it occasionally.

The Lord does this same thing with us on a personal level. He may, for example, take us through a season in which He emphasizes patience in a predominate way. When He has established this fruit of the Spirit in us, He can then approach it in a more balanced way.

We must be careful with this thing called balance. It is such a relative concept. What is balance for me at this time, may not be for you. What my fellowship currently needs, yours may not. What the Church in America needs, Argentina may not. What my marriage needs, yours may not. It seems contradictory, but sometimes God has to get us *out of balance* for a while to get us *in balance*. If we're not careful, our quest for balance keeps us out of balance.

I am a firm believer in sound doctrine. It is imperative for the Church. But balance is not rooted in a doctrine, creed or belief system. I know individuals who have the basic doctrines of the church down to a science. They can dot every "i" and cross every "t," but their spiritual lives are out of balance. They can study all day, but couldn't sit in God's presence quietly worshiping or praying for two hours without being bored to tears. Please don't think you are balanced spiritually because you are sound in doctrine.

It is possible for us, as it was for the Pharisees, to "search the Scriptures" (John 5:39), learn them well and still not know God. John the Baptist didn't know half of what they knew and would have been considered weird to most in his day, but he was more balanced than any of them. Why? His "imbalanced" life was God's "balance" for him. *Balance is not measured by normality*.

A desire for balance can be nothing more than a desire for respectability. But if we're considered normal by the world, we're probably out of balance biblically. The same thing is true concerning much of the Church world. Less than 20 percent of Christians in America tithe. Few pray and read their Bibles daily. Fewer still fast, and most rarely ever share their faith. Be careful whom you allow to define balance for you.

Balance is rooted in a personal relationship with Christ. The more radically committed we are to Him, the more balanced we are. Someone once said a radical Christian might just be someone who loves Christ more than we do. Love Him passionately and allow Him to determine what is right for you. If it is weeping, do it. If laughter, so be it. We are not to seek manifestations, nor are we to fear or avoid them. We would be wise to heed the advice given to George Whitefield concerning strange manifestations in his meetings:

> When similar things began to occur in Whitefield's meetings, he was inclined to silence the people or have them removed. But Lady Huntingdon, whom Whitefield greatly respected, saw things otherwise. This was the counsel she gave to the greatest preacher of that century: "You are making a mistake. Don't be wiser than God. Let them cry out; it will do a great deal more good than your preaching." Are we also trying to be wiser than God, or can we trust Him to do His work in His way?[1]

Why all this discussion of balance? Because it becomes a big issue in any season of revival. Strange things happen. People fall down. They laugh, they cry. Some shake under the influence of the Holy Spirit, a few get drunk. Others groan, some cry out. Many dance and leap for joy. Not much balance there.

179

—

Manifestations grab our attention,
but our goal must be to save people, transform
lives and give hope to the hopeless.

—

In Christ's meetings they tore up roofs, climbed trees, crawled through crowds, cried out interrupting the teaching, wept on His feet and poured bottles of perfume on Him. Demons cried out. Meetings lasted for days—not much balance there either.

When revival begins, the key to balance is not insisting on holding to our traditionally boring services. The key is to allow the Holy Spirit to do what He desires and emphasize the truths He wishes, without pitching our tents there forever, and without abandoning everything else He has taught us up to that point. A new understanding or revelation is to be *added to* our former knowledge, not *replace* it.

Manifestations grab our attention, but they are not the truths we build on. They are not an end and must never be the goal of what we do. Seeking them leads to error. They arrest the attention of the church and the world, so God can then do other things. The "other things" are the goal—saving people, transforming lives, healing homes and marriages and giving hope to the hopeless, just to name a few.

As Michael Brown states:

> Manifestations in past revivals were the *result* of the preaching, while many of today's manifestations are the *object* of the meeting, becoming the *focus* of the teaching, the *proof* of the praying and the *showcase* of the service.[2]
>
> It's so easy to get caught up in the fervor of revival, in the excitement of the manifestations, that we forget about something critical: God wants the heart, and through the Word of God, He probes the heart and changes the heart. The excitement will pass, and the manifestations will wane. But if the trumpet has been sounded, if the awakening cry has been raised, if the burden of the Lord has been delivered, if the radical call to follow Jesus in a radical way has gone forth, that will determine just how deeply individuals will be changed. *The Word is the road map for the revival's future.*[3]

Those of us who believe God still does unusual, supernatural things in our day have brought much of our persecution on ourselves. As Brown alludes, we have made peripheral happenings sacred truths, trying to make doctrines of them. In our hunger to see supernatural events, we have manufactured counterfeits in the flesh. We have tried to make the exception normal.

An example would be someone blowing on a person, the Holy Spirit using it to accomplish something, and we then establish a blowing ministry. Another example is someone being healed through a prayer cloth. Someone else might come along and abuse the practice, making a fortune selling them. While both of these things happened in Scripture, they are not to become gimmicks or attention-getters. The cause of these errors ranges from outright greed and hypocrisy to sincere deception.

Talk about extremes, I once saw a person healed of a malignant tumor when a minister hit her in the stomach. I don't intend to pattern my ministry after this, however. Jesus spit on a man's eyes and they were healed. I have no intention of doing this either. Signs and wonders are for signs and wonders, not for imitating as patterns.

It's Not Because They're Out of Balance

One phenomenon of the Holy Spirit that has caused us charismatics a lot of grief is what we call being "slain in the Spirit." Again, we have brought much of the reproach on ourselves. First of all, this is unwise terminology for it. "Falling under the power" would be much better.

Nor is there much scriptural basis for something that so many make so prevalent. The Bible does speak of some falling down when impacted by God (see Rev. 1:17; Dan. 8:17) and of others who "could not stand" to minister (1 Kings 8:11). There are not a lot of biblical references to this phenomenon, however, and none that speak of being "slain in the Spirit."

Nevertheless, the practice isn't new. Almost all revivals in church history have seen this manifestation take place. Dr. Martyn Lloyd-Jones once said in a sermon on revival:

Under the influence of this mighty power, people may literally fall to the ground under conviction of sin, or even faint, and remain in a state of unconsciousness...there are people who seem to go into trances. They may be seated or they may be standing, and they are looking into the distance, obviously seeing something, and yet they are completely unconscious and unaware of their surroundings.

They do not seem to be able to hear anything, nor to see anything that may be happening round and about them.[4]

In *The Biography of Barton W. Stone* (1847) there is an interesting quote concerning the manifestations accompanying the Second Great Awakening, including people falling down:

> During the progress of this revival, scenes were exhibited somewhat extraordinary. It was not unusual to have a large proportion of the congregation prostrate on the floor, and in some instances they lost the use of their limbs.... Screams, groans, shouts, hosannas, notes of grief and joy, all at the same time, were not unfrequently heard throughout their vast assemblies.[5]

There is nothing new about people falling under God's power, but just what is happening when this takes place? What is valid, and what is invalid? Are there times when some truly are "slain" or unconscious? Are there abuses? I am certainly not an expert on this or any manifestation of the Holy Spirit, but I have observed much. Here are some thoughts to consider.

Most people who fall down in Pentecostal or charismatic services while being prayed for could stay on their feet if they wanted. A few are truly "overcome" by the Holy Spirit, but I believe they are the exception. It is, however, sometimes easier to receive lying on the floor. Why? For several reasons:

1. Sometimes it is good to allow more time for the Holy Spirit to minister. Several minutes, a half hour, an hour or even more is sometimes beneficial to "soak" in the river of His Spirit. Simply remaining in God's presence, allowing Him to minister to us, is healthy. This is much easier sitting or lying down.

2. It is also easier for most to receive ministry from the Holy Spirit without a lot of distraction. Thus, it becomes easier with one's eyes closed. Standing for a prolonged

    time with closed eyes is difficult, however. It is easier
    sitting or lying down.

3. Another reason it is sometimes advantageous is because
    it is easier to receive ministry when totally relaxed. This,
    too, is hard to do while standing still for any length of
    time. It is much easier to relax while lying prostrate.

"So why do they have to *fall?*" you may ask. They don't,
except for the few who are truly overcome by God's power. It
would probably be simpler if people would start by sitting,
kneeling or lying down. I have been in churches where this is
done. Those receiving prayer who like to "soak" in the river for
a while simply lay down from the start. Others knelt. It worked
wonderfully and was much less chaotic than it sometimes is with
people falling.

Of course, it's also much less dramatic, which is, I believe, a
part of our charismatic problem. Often, we are so hungry to see
God move in dramatic, supernatural ways, we end up operating
in the flesh. This creates confusion, disillusionment and division.
When confronted about it, we charismatics typically defend it in
an effort to "contend for the faith." It would be much wiser to
admit our weaknesses and make every effort to correct them.

Another unfortunate happening is people sometimes feel pressured to fall simply because so many around them have fallen.
After all, no one wants to be the "unspiritual" one left standing.
This happened to me in a meeting once. Many years ago a gentleman brought me to the front of a large gathering to pray for me.
He liked to see people fall. He blew on them, touched them, even
"threw" them blessings. After several unsuccessful attempts to
"slay" me, I finally fell down, just to get out of the embarrassing
situation. I shouldn't have, but it seemed like the easiest way out
at the time.

As happened with me, I'm sure individuals sometimes feel
pressured to fall down by the person ministering to them.
Sometimes the pressure is literal. This manipulation is unfortunate.
In our fellowship, we train our altar workers that a gentle touch on

183

the forehead is all that is permitted. I know what it is like to be pushed down and don't like it.

There are also occasions when the individual ministering may feel pressured to get people to fall. If five people in a row have fallen, and the sixth doesn't, it is easy to find yourself asking, *I wonder why this one didn't fall? Is it my fault or his/hers? Should I pray longer, more fervently?* We must guard against this.

If not careful, manipulation can result. A little more pressure, perhaps, or some encouraging words. "Just relax and receive. That's it, relax." Nothing is wrong with encouraging people to relax and receive, as long as it isn't a suggestion to fall down. I fear at times our manipulation could even be directed toward the Holy Spirit through louder, more fervent praying.

We must guard against a mentality that must see something physically to believe God is ministering to someone spiritually. At times, people on their feet receive more from God than the person on the floor next to them. We shouldn't care what position a person is in while receiving from God.

My suggestion is if some want to talk to God on a kneeling bench, let them. If others want to stand or walk, great. If still others prefer a prostrate position, let them receive from God on the floor. If God chooses to knock a few down, well, I guess that's His business.

In any fresh outpouring of the Holy Spirit, God's power will be manifested. This may result in healings, shaking, laughter, people falling down and perhaps other phenomena. We must allow Him to move as He desires. During these times, those of us in leadership have the responsibility to govern without controlling.

We must guard against extremes of the flesh while allowing the extremes of the Spirit. We should not seek physical manifestations, nor should we be afraid or ashamed of them when they occur. Let's clean up the abuses but not throw away the good with the bad.

Are you ready for new wine?

Notes

1. Michael L. Brown, *From Holy Laughter to Holy Fire* (Shippensburg, PA: Destiny Image Publishers, Inc., 1996), p. 125.
2. Ibid., p. 21.
3. Ibid., p. 243.
4. Richard M. Riss, "Evangelical Heroes Speak," *Destiny Image Digest*, vol. 5, no. 3 (Fall 1997), p. 27.
5. Ibid., pp. 28, 29.

CHAPTER TWELVE

Devotion Finds a Way

I don't like losing things. Usually, I deal with it pretty well—unless, of course, it is something that makes me late, such as car keys. Though I am unusually spiritual, weighted down with the fruit of the Spirit, I have been known to grow impatient on occasion when someone else moves my keys from where I placed them. How else could my wife always be the one to find them?! I don't care if they were in the pocket of the coat I wore yesterday. *I* certainly didn't leave them there.

Then there is the remote for the television—not that I ever watch it. I'm far too spiritual for that. How many places can there possibly be in one room to hide the thing? My kids are creative geniuses. There is no other explanation for such inventive concealment. We never did find one remote that disappeared!

Then there was the science project we lost. Well, it wasn't really lost. *The dogs ate it!* Yeah, I know, but this time they really did. It was a project testing cheeses, trying to determine which kind molded the most and the fastest. We were finished with the project; all the ugly cheese was glued beautifully on the poster board, the explanations scripted nicely by each moldy slice. Three glorious weeks of watching cheese mold, and it was finally finished. The display was carefully leaned against the wall, and off we went to a Wednesday night church service.

While we were gone, the dogs had a party. Poster board was scattered everywhere, along with a few morsels of the moldiest cheese. When I walked into the room, my daughter Sarah was angry, my wife was distressed, the dogs were hiding, and my other daughter, Hannah, was just trying to stay out of everyone's way.

I tried to minister peace to everyone. "They didn't mean anything by it," I said. "They were just doing what came naturally to them."

Sarah gave me a look that was similar to the one she was giving the dogs. Ceci gave me a look that was a cross between sarcasm and pity. "Brilliant," she said. "Now we all feel better. We'll just tell the school the dogs were hungry and did what came naturally to them."

Not to be denied an opportunity to show I'm smarter than dogs, I tried again. *A little humor is what we need*, I thought. "I bet it was funny seeing the look on those dogs' faces when they tasted that mold," I said through a small chuckle. "It always helps, Sarah, to see the humor in situations such as this. If you can laugh about it, you'll feel better."

She cried even harder, mumbling something about a weird sense of humor.

Then it hit me. "Honesty is always the best policy," I instructed. "I will simply go tell your principal the dogs ate your science project. He will understand, and everything will be okay."

I went to the school the following morning, after having slept with the dogs, and explained to the principal what had happened. "Our dogs ate Sarah's science project," I said. You can imagine my relief when he laughed. "Finally," I said, "someone else who sees the humor in it!"

Later that day I was looking for the remote. "The dogs ate it," Sarah informed me with a devious smile.

"That's not funny!" I said. Some people have a weird sense of humor.

Running on Empty

No, I don't like losing things—keys, remotes, directions, pens. (I just lost another Cross.) But I especially hate losing the anointing and presence of God. I don't like it when the fire goes out or the flow of the river wanes. I find it disconcerting when the cutting edge becomes the dull edge. It can, however, and probably does happen to all of us.

We have already discussed some problems that aborted portions of what God wanted to accomplish in the charismatic movement. This chapter approaches the same general subject on a personal level: What is it that causes the river to dry up on an individual basis?

Interestingly enough, success itself can be the culprit. What a touch of irony—success can make us unsuccessful. Frequently it is the breeding ground for pride, burnout, complacency and a host of other deadly diseases. Remember, the best way to lose a move of God is to lose God in the move.

> One New Year's Day, in the Tournament of Roses parade, a beautiful float suddenly sputtered and quit. It was out of gas. The whole parade was held up until someone could get a can of gas.
>
> The amusing thing was this float represented the Standard Oil Company. With its vast oil resources, its truck was out of gas.[1]

Often we who have within us the well of salvation, the river of life, fail to drink from it. Like the Standard Oil float, we can run out of gas.

How can we prevent this? How do we stay fresh, sharp and alive and ward off burnout? How do we keep from losing God in the move?

I was just yesterday made aware of a wonderful and very successful pastor in our city who stood before his congregation last Sunday and announced a sabbatical. He is nearly burned out and can barely function. I know this man. He's a great pastor and a true man of God. I'm praying for a great renewal in his life. It appears that he recognized the symptoms quickly enough to avert disaster.

In his powerful book, *Intimacy with the Almighty*, Charles

Swindoll tells of a clergyman who approached him with these words: "Nobody around me knows this, but I'm operating on fumes. I am lonely, hollow, shallow, enslaved to a schedule that never lets up."[2] As they embraced and prayed, the pastor wept with deep, heaving sobs. This man is not the exception. I'm told that 50 percent of all pastors in America considered leaving the ministry in 1997.

Daniel 7:25 alerts us that one of Satan's strategies is to "wear down the saints of the Highest One." Been there, done that, have that scar.

"You Are Never Safe Here Except on Your Knees"

The Lord told Joshua not to be dismayed as he faced the awesome task of leading Israel (see Joshua 1:9). "Dismayed" is translated from the Hebrew word, *chathath*, meaning "to break." Zodhiates says "The meaning ranges from a literal breaking to abstract destruction, to demoralization, and finally to panic."[3] He likens it to the concept we use in our times of "cracking under the stress."[4] God was telling Joshua to *chill out*, to not let the stress get to him.

God knew it would be difficult. Possessing the land can be more demanding than roaming in the wilderness. One involves the stress of stagnation and failure, the other the pressures of progress. Both are equally dangerous.

How do we keep from cracking under the stress? What maintains freshness? Joy? The anointing? Can the river truly be fun, as it was when God put me in it? In this chapter, I want to share what I believe to be the most important principle we must walk in to maintain freshness—a truth that will ensure we won't lose God in the move, but instead move with God. It is simple, yet sometimes extremely difficult. When we manage to walk in this vital understanding, however, the results are rewarding.

The principle I'm referring to is to place greater importance on *spending time with* the Lord than to *ministering for* Him. It is prioritizing relationship over service, worship over work. As simple and basic as this sounds, it is by far the most difficult challenge of our Christian life. Our great propensity for "*doing* over *being*" often causes us to walk in a performance mind-set. It is difficult for us to believe God wants *us* more than our service.

We ministers are just as guilty as anyone else. I sometimes feel there is actually a subconscious guilt that comes to those in ministry when significant blocks of time are given to simply waiting, listening, resting, reading, praying—activities that should be our highest priority.

In *Touch and Live*, George Vandeman writes:

A young stranger to the Alps was making his first climb, accompanied by two stalwart guides. It was a steep, hazardous ascent. But he felt secure with one guide ahead and one following. For hours they climbed. And now, breathless, they reached for those rocks protruding through the snow above them—the summit.

The guide ahead wished to let the stranger have the first glorious view of heaven and earth, and moved aside to let him go first. Forgetting the gales that would blow across those summit rocks, the young man leaped to his feet. But the chief guide dragged him down. "On your knees, sir!" he shouted. "You are never safe here except on your knees."[5]

In this world where we are buffeted by the gale-force winds of sin, temptation, busyness, frenzy and stress, we are never safe except when we are "on our knees," spending quality time with our heavenly Father. This is especially true when we are cresting mountains.

Courting God

As John Stott stated, "Our greatest claim to nobility is our created capacity to know God, to be in personal relationship with him, to love him and to worship him. Indeed, we are most truly human when we are on our knees before our Creator."[6]

Proverbs 3:5,6 tells us "Trust in the Lord with all your heart, and do not lean on your own understanding. In all your ways acknowledge Him, and He will make your paths straight." One possible metaphoric meaning to these words is interesting and very pertinent to our subject.

The word "ways," translated from the Hebrew word *derek*, means literally a "way, road, journey, manner, work."[7] More often than not, however, it is used metaphorically, referring to the actions and behavior of people.[8] It "has the unusual sense of 'sexual favors' in Jeremiah 3:13 and Proverbs 31:3." *Derek* is the word chosen for the act of *courting* in Proverbs 30:19.[9]

Imagine that, courting God.

Consistent with this relational theme, the word "acknowledge" comes from *yada*, which is the Old Testament word for knowing someone in a very intimate—even physical—way.[10] Adam knew (*yada*) Eve, and she conceived (see Genesis 4:1). Using these concepts and definitions we could paraphrase Proverbs 3:6, "In all your ways, court God; seek intimacy with Him."

In the "ways" of ministry and life in general, many things are courted: success, advancement, fame, other people, glory, money, favor and a myriad of other goals we humans strive to reach. Gordon Dahl aptly said, "Most middle-class Americans tend to worship their work, to work at their play, and to play at their worship."[11] Seeking and loving God with all of our hearts, souls, minds and strength is often lost in the melee. *And so is our source of strength and life*. Nothing will cause the flow of the river to abate more quickly than this common mistake.

We must drink daily from the fountain. Sometimes I feel like the small child in the "Family Circus" cartoon who ran up to his mother exclaiming, "I need a hug, Mommy. I used up the last one."[12] It doesn't take long to use up our spiritual hugs.

What happens when we pursue God? Courting Him in all of our ways or work (*derek*) leads to intimacy (*yada*), which leads to *conception*. Just as Adam knew Eve and she conceived, as we

seek and wait on God, He speaks to us. When He does, His word
or seed (see 1 Pet. 1:23) is planted in us, and *that which is born
from our lives is now of Him*. Our visions, plans, methods, ministries, relationships—all can then be born of God, *not of ourselves*.

God isn't into surrogate parenting—someone else carrying
His seed of revelation for us. He wants to sow it into us *personally*. He wants to breathe His word into our hearts. Insights we

—

Tapes, seminars and books must not take the place of hearing from God PERSONALLY and DIRECTLY.

—

193

receive from others are good and valid, but if that is the only way
we receive, we're living far below our privileges.

He is not into artificial insemination either—placing His seed
in us without relationship. Tapes, seminars and books are all
good, but they must not take the place of hearing from God *personally* and *directly*. Conferences where the word of God is
flowing wonderfully can become nothing more than a sterile lab-
oratory of information if we're not careful. Under the guise of
not reinventing the wheel, we don't reinvent the revelation
either. Someone else's will do just fine.

The problem is not receiving teaching through another—this
is obviously one of the ways God does it—the problem is when
that becomes the primary source of our information. We cannot
live on another's revelation. We must hear from God ourselves.
And when He speaks to us through someone else, we still must
pray and meditate over the information (courting God) until it
becomes a personal word of revelation to us.

As strange as it may sound, we can even become "pregnant"
with someone else's revelation and, yes, birth another person's
child. The Church is filled with people trying to walk in someone

else's revelation, vision, ideas and methods. And we wonder why so much of what we do produces so little fruit. Every time I see another church growth conference advertised, I cringe. It isn't that the principles shared are wrong. They probably worked well for the person sharing them. But each of us must allow the Holy Spirit to show us how to apply truth to our personal situation. The method that worked for one may not work for another. Principles can be applied many ways and at many timings. What is *God* saying to *me* now? must be the question we ask ourselves.

We cannot clone revival, church growth or any other form of ministry. *Revival is not produced, it is born!* The river is not just *about* God, it flows *from* Him. We can run our churches and ministries from the boardroom or the prayer room. The first produces the works of man, the other births a move of God.

Going Around in Circles

I don't like it when God sends me to the gospel of Luke, chapter 10. My response is usually a profound "Uh-oh." I know what's there. Luke 10:38-42 is the story of Mary and Martha—or should I say of Mary and most of the leadership of the church. As I feel drawn to or am reminded of this passage, I know the Father is about to correct me for prioritizing ministry *for* Him over ministry *to* Him.

I have a love-hate relationship with this report. I love the Mary syndrome, hate the Martha syndrome. I want the Mary life but do more of the Martha life—right down to the complaining.

Let's take a closer look at the passage. While I'm certain many of you are familiar with it, some of the truths found there have largely gone unnoticed.

Now as they were traveling along, He entered a certain village; and a woman named Martha welcomed Him into her home. And she had a sister called Mary, who moreover was listening to the Lord's word, seated at His feet.

But Martha was distracted with all her preparations; and she came up to Him, and said, "Lord, do You not care that my sister has left me to do all the serving alone? Then tell her to help me."

But the Lord answered and said to her, "Martha, Martha, you are worried and bothered about so many things; but only a few things are necessary, really only one, for Mary has chosen the good part, which shall not be taken away from her" (Luke 10:38-42).

When Mary was seated at the feet of the Lord and Martha was busy in the kitchen, the passage says Martha "was distracted with all her preparations" (v. 40). The word "distracted" comes from the Greek verb *perispao*. It means to literally "drag around in circles."[13] The word for "preparations" is the New Testament word for "ministry," *diakonia*—the same word we would use for a person in the ministry. Even pure ministry for Jesus can become a weight we drag around. It's called the "treadmill anointing," and it isn't from God.

Several years ago I was going through a difficult period in my life. Al Straarup, a dear friend of mine, called me and said, "I was praying for you with a friend this morning and God gave him a picture."

I thought, *Thank you, Jesus. Here comes my answer.*

Al continued, "There was a circle on the ground." I was ready for a great revelation—the wheel in the middle of a wheel or something! "You were walking on that circle," he said.

I replied, "Yeah? Yeah?"

He said, "That's it. You were just walking in circles."

"That's my word from God?" I asked.

He responded, "Yeah, that's it. Sorry."

I hung up the phone and said, "Thanks a lot, God." But the more I thought about it, the more I realized its accuracy. *I guess it's true*, I reasoned. *That's what I'm doing—walking in circles; busy, but going nowhere.* I stepped off that treadmill and into the presence of the Lord.

In an interview for *Today's Christian Woman*, writer and speaker Carol Kent says:

One day when [my son] Jason was young, we were eating breakfast together. I had on an old pair of slacks and a fuzzy old sweater. He flashed his baby blues at me over his cereal bowl and said, "Mommy, you look so pretty today."

I didn't even have makeup on! So I said, "Honey, why would you say I look pretty today? Normally I'm dressed up in a suit and high heels."

And he said, "When you look like that, I know you're going some place; but when you look like this, I know you're all mine."[14]

I do much of my praying in a woods. I love to walk there for hours, communing with the Lord. I usually wear grubby jeans, old boots, t-shirts or sweatshirts depending on the weather, hats and other worn-out, non-professional attire. When I go to the office, I change into my nicer clothes. I think God prefers me in my grungy uniform. When He sees me dressed that way, He knows I'm all His.

My experience in the woods is often like that described by A.W. Tozer. "There are occasions when for hours I lay prostrate before God without saying a word of prayer or a word of praise— I just gaze on Him and worship."[15] Sometimes no words are needed as we enjoy one another's company.

There's Nothing Complicated About Relationship with Christ

Ecclesiastes 7:29 in the *Good News Bible, Today's English Version* says, "God made us plain and simple, but we have made ourselves very complicated." I've always felt the latter part of the verse was true about women, and I'm told that the first half is true of us men. But I now accept that it is all true of all of us.

I don't know about you, but I can complicate almost any

problem, regardless of how simple it might be, making it huge and complex. And I don't like it when someone else tries to trivialize it, or gives me some simple plan to fix it. Somehow, I just seem to feel more important when I have big problems with complicated solutions. I'm an Ecclesiastes 7 kind of guy!

—

When it's time for relationship with Jesus,
don't share His time with anyone or anything
—not even cooking for Him!

—

We must de-complicate things. Paul said to the church at Corinth, "But I am afraid, lest as the serpent deceived Eve by his craftiness, your minds should be led astray from the *simplicity* and purity of devotion to Christ" (2 Cor. 11:3, italics mine). Life can be very complicated; so can theology. At times, if we're not careful, things can get downright confusing. But the Lord impresses on my heart time and time again, *There is nothing complicated about relationship with Me.* It was A.W. Tozer who said:

> Now, as always, God [discloses] himself to "babes" and hides himself in thick darkness from the wise and the prudent. We must *simplify* our approach to him. We must strip down to essentials (and they will be found to be blessedly few). We must put away all effort to impress, and come with the guileless candor of childhood. If we do this, without doubt God will quickly respond.[16]

In 2 Corinthians 11:3 "simplify" is the word *haplotes.* In addition to simplicity, the word means "singleness, without dissimulation"[17] or "the opposite of duplicity."[18] The verse is saying that, in our devotion to Christ, we must not be double-minded. We must guard against anything causing dissimulation, division or a watering down. It is okay to be multifaceted in our gifts and activities, but not in our approach to relationship with Jesus. Everything else must shut down when it is time for this. Don't share His time with anyone or anything, not even cooking for Him.

After the circumference of her ministry is revealed in Luke 10:40, the Lord then said to Martha (who was standing in proxy for me), "Martha, Martha, you are worried and bothered about so many things" (v. 41). "Worried" here is the word *merimnao*, which has in its root concept the idea of dividing or parting.[19] A similar word, *merismas*, is used in Hebrews 4:12 to describe the Word of God making a "division of soul and spirit." The worry in Martha was caused by a division in her mind—a divided mind. She *wanted* to be listening to the Lord, she was even jealous of Mary, but Martha was just *too busy*, going in too many directions.

Someone once gave me a two-billed cap—one points left, the other right—imprinted with the words, "I'm their leader, which way did they go?" How sadly appropriate. At times I think I need two of me. Is this God's plan for me? Or have I wrongly defined words such as "calling," "urgency" and "important"? It seems that God isn't the only one with a plan for my life. Everybody has one for me!

Get Out of the Kitchen!

The word "bothered" the Lord used when referring to Martha is just as revelatory and painful as "worried." It is the word *turbazo*, which comes from the Latin word *turba*, meaning "a crowd."[20] Martha's mind was too crowded, as is my life and schedule. Even God was crowded out. *Serving Him wasn't, but courting Him was.*

Webster says "disturb," "perturb," and "turbulent" are all derivatives of this same word.[21] (This is getting worse, isn't it?) My life gets so crowded I become disturbed. Perturbed comes next. With ministry? Yes, and with life in general. And turbulent? Oh yes, turbulent.

I do a lot of flying, and when I think of turbulence, I think of a rough flight. I've seen it turbulent enough to make people throw up. But let's don't go *there*. Suffice it to say I'm getting sick of the Martha syndrome! I'm ready for a little more frolicking with Jesus in His river. I'm ready for some beach time.

The point is this: Life, even the life of ministry, has a way of crowding out God. My mind becomes divided, and the next thing I know I'm on the merciless treadmill of busyness. I'm productive, but I'm not birthing. Ministry is flowing from a stagnant cistern in me, not a bubbling well of life. The river? I don't think so. Not even a trickle at this point. Everything generated is natural, not supernatural. Or just as bad, I'm birthing, but it's someone else's baby! What a scary thought.

I said it once, let me say it again: *Revival is not produced, it is born.* Born in the living room, not the kitchen. And what is born there will be of Him.

What is the solution to our Martha tendency? Placing a higher priority on listening than on ministering...being like Mary. The passage tells us she was seated, listening to His word. Like Martha, doesn't that just make you mad! Mary wasn't scurrying here and there, trying to catch a word or two when possible. No, Jesus had her undivided attention. In essence, Mary was saying, "If He wants anything to eat, He had better quit talking. Because until He does, I'm not leaving this spot."

Why did Martha feel different? What was the problem? Jesus spent a lot of time here in her home. He stayed there whenever in the area. Could it be that Martha had grown a little too familiar with Him? Does this ever happen to us? Does Christ lose His ability to impress us?

In *Christianity Today*, Philip Yancey writes:

I remember my first visit to Old Faithful in Yellowstone National Park. Rings of Japanese and German tourists surrounded the geyser, their video cameras trained like weapons on the famous hole in the ground. A large, digital clock stood beside the spot, predicting 24 minutes until the next eruption.

My wife and I passed the countdown in the dining room of Old Faithful Inn overlooking the geyser. When the digital clock reached one minute, we, along with every other diner, left our seats and rushed to the windows to see the big, wet event.

I noticed that immediately, as if on signal, a crew of busboys and waiters descended on the tables to refill water glasses and clear away dirty dishes. When the geyser went off, we tourists oohed and aahed and clicked our cameras; a few spontaneously applauded. But, glancing back over my shoulder, I saw that not a single waiter or busboy—not even those who had finished their chores—looked out the huge windows. Old Faithful, grown entirely too familiar, had lost its power to impress them.[22]

I'm afraid this describes many Christians' relationships with the One we call Faithful and True. We've known Him so long, become so accustomed to Him, well, you know....

Don't ever stop being impressed with Jesus!

It's interesting that those in this story who had lost their wonder over Old Faithful were "kitchen people"—just like Martha. Get out of the kitchen once in a while! Slow down! STOP!

Do you ever listen and not really *hear*? The word "listening" in Greek is the word *akouo*, which means not only to hear, but to understand. One definition said, "To understand, hear with the ear of the mind."[23]

Interestingly enough, the word for "obey," *hupakouo*, comes from the same word. The prefix *hupo* means "under," making the literal meaning of this word "hear under." For all you bottom-liners, here is the point. (Perhaps I should say, "*Hear* is the point.") The biblical concept of obedience is *hearing and understanding* someone, then bringing your will *under* that person's will. It doesn't take a genius to figure out you can't hear *under* until you *hear*. Mary was hearing (*akouo*), so she could obey (*hupakouo*).

In the phrase "listening to the Lord's *word*" (Luke 10:39), the Greek word *logos* is used, not *rhema*. If *rhema* had been used, it could mean she merely heard the words He was saying. *Logos* does include this, but it also embodies *the message* the words are communicating. Our English word "logic" is derived from it.

Again, it is clear Mary was not only listening, she was under-standing what He was saying. His logic or reasoning was coming across. Is it any wonder she's the one who washed His feet, anointing Him for burial.

Choose the Good Part

In the book, *When You're All Out of Noodles*, Ken Jones conveys a lesson he learned one day at the office.

> [When I walked into my office] I noticed something I had never seen before. It was round, about the size of a dessert plate, and plugged into the wall, giving out a constant noise. It wasn't a loud noise, just constant. *What in the world is that thing?* I thought as I stopped to stare.
>
> I finally asked the receptionist about it. She said, "It's an ambient noise generator. If it's too quiet in here, we can distinguish the voices in the counseling offices, and we want to protect their privacy. So we bought the noise generator to cover the voices."
>
> Her explanation made perfect sense to me, but didn't it have to be louder to mask the conversations? I asked. "No," she said. "The constancy of the sound tricks the ear so that what is being said can't be distinguished."
>
> *Interesting*, I thought. *Very interesting.* One kind of noise to cover the sound of another. It made me think and pray.
>
> *No wonder, Lord. No wonder I strain to hear what you have to say to me....The constancy of sound—little noises, soft, inward, ambient thoughts and fears and attitudes—tricks the ears of my inner man and masks your still, small voice.*
>
> God isn't silent. We just have trouble hearing him.[24]

Martha's ambient noise generator was her service for Christ. Incredible! The constancy of sound—dishes rattling, cupboards banging, silverware clanging—all was too constant. Mine is counseling, sermon preparation, preaching, letters, books—all good stuff, but muffling the voice of the Master.

Mary didn't have one of these contraptions. Therefore, she heard and understood. This is why Jesus said of her, "Mary has chosen the good part, which shall not be taken away from her" (v. 42). "Good part" is the word *agathos*. It is contrasted to another word for "good" in Greek, *kalos*, which means something is "constitutionally good"[25] or, in other words, is made well. But *kalos* doesn't necessarily imply any practical usefulness or benefit. It may simply look good. Nothing is wrong with it, but it may not have any practical purpose.

On the other hand, *agathos*—the "good part"—is a word that means "good and profitable; useful; beneficial."[26] It is often translated "good works." The Lord is saying, "If you spend time waiting upon Me, seated at My feet listening, it puts something of substance in you. You will not only look good, but you'll also be *good for something*." We often look good, but lack anointing. We must wait in His presence until we're filled with His Spirit and the ability to minister true life.

It is significant that Mary *chose* the good part. I have found that if I don't make the *choice* to prioritize waiting on the Lord, many other pressures and activities will make the decision for me. I can choose to manage my life based on God's priorities for me, or I can be ruled by needs, circumstances, pressures and other issues of life.

Make a decision today to be as Mary. Prioritize listening over ministering. Slow down, be quiet and wait upon Him. Get off the circle! Unplug the generator. He is ready to speak to you, to impregnate you with His words. Let nothing stop you.

Alvin Straight, age 73, lived in Laurens, Iowa. His brother, age 80, lived several hundred miles away in Blue River, Wisconsin. According to the Associated Press, Alvin's brother had suffered a stroke, and Alvin wanted to see him, but he had a transportation problem. He didn't have a driver's license because his eyesight was bad and he apparently had an aversion to taking a plane, train or bus.

But Alvin didn't let that stop him. In 1994 he climbed aboard his 1966 John Deere tractor lawn mower and drove it all the way to Blue River, Wisconsin.

Devotion finds a way.[27]

If true revival comes to us in America, if the river begins to flow with great depth and force, there will be much to distract us from its source. If we allow this, the fruit will be temporary and the joy of the river will fade. We must choose "the good part, which shall not be taken away."

The birth of Tommy, a healthy, beautiful son, was an event for celebration, and as time went by, it seemed as though every day brought another reason to celebrate the gift of Tommy's life. He was sweet, thoughtful, fun-loving and a joy to be around.

One day when Tommy was about five years old, he and Debbie, his mother, were driving to the neighborhood mall. As is the way with children, out of nowhere, Tommy asked, "Mom, how old were you when I was born?"

"Thirty-six, Tommy. Why?" Debbie asked, wondering what his little mind was contemplating.

"What a shame!" Tommy responded.

"What do you mean?" Debbie inquired, more than a little puzzled. Looking at her with love-filled eyes, Tommy said, "Just think of all those years we didn't know each other."[28]

May we, like Tommy, become so infatuated, so mesmerized, so taken with the Lord we can't stand to be away from Him. May we loathe the days before we met Him. Let us tenaciously fight for quality time at His feet and never cease to be impressed with "Faithful and True."

Thank you, Mary.

Notes

1. Craig Brian Larson, *Illustrations for Preaching and Teaching* (Grand Rapids: Baker Books, 1993), p. 181.
2. Charles R. Swindoll, *Intimacy with the Almighty* (Dallas: Word Publishing, Inc., 1996), pp. 9, 10.
3. Spiros Zodhiates, *Hebrew-Greek Key Study Bible—New American Standard* (Chattanooga: AMG Publishers, 1984; revised edition, 1990), p. 1729.
4. Ibid, p. 1729.
5. Larson, *Illustrations for Preaching and Teaching*, p. 281.
6. Edward K. Rowell, *Quotes & Idea Starters for Preaching and Teaching* (Grand Rapids: Baker Books, 1996), p. 183.
7. R. Laird Harris, Gleason L. Archer Jr. and Bruce K. Waltke, *Theological Wordbook of the Old Testament* (Chicago: Moody Press, 1980), p. 196.
8. Ibid., p. 197.
9. Ibid., p. 198.
10. Zodhiates, *Hebrew-Greek Key Study Bible—New American Standard*, p. 1720.
11. Rowell, *Quotes & Idea Starters for Preaching and Teaching*, p. 181.
12. Jack Canfield and Mark Victor Hansen, *A Third Serving of Chicken Soup for the Soul* (Deerfield Beach, FL: Health Communications, Inc., 1996), p. 99.
13. James Strong, *The New Strong's Exhaustive Concordance of the Bible* (Nashville: Thomas Nelson Publishers, 1990), ref. no. 4049.
14. Craig Brian Larson, *Contemporary Illustrations for Preachers, Teachers and Writers* (Grand Rapids: Baker Books, 1996), p. 70.
15. Michael L. Brown, *From Holy Laughter to Holy Fire* (Shippensburg, PA: Destiny Image Publishers, Inc., 1996), p. 186.
16. Rowell, *Quotes & Idea Starters for Preaching and Teaching*, p. 21.
17. Strong, *The New Strong's Exhaustive Concordance of the Bible*, ref. no. 572.
18. Zodhiates, *Hebrew-Greek Key Study Bible—New American Standard*, p. 1808.
19. Spiros Zodhiates, *The Complete Word Study Dictionary* (Iowa Falls, Iowa: Word Bible Publishers, Inc., 1992), pp. 961, 962.
20. Strong, *The New Strong's Exhaustive Concordance of the Bible*, ref. no. 5182.
21. *The Consolidated-Webster Encyclopedic Dictionary* (Chicago: Consolidated Book Publishers, 1954), pp. 220, 534, 778.
22. Larson, *Contemporary Illustrations for Preachers, Teachers and Writers*, p. 68.
23. Zodhiates, *Hebrew-Greek Key Study Bible—New American Standard*, p. 1802.

24. Larson, *Contemporary Illustrations for Preachers, Teachers and Writers*, p. 101.
25. Zodhiates, *Hebrew-Greek Key Study Bible—New American Standard*, p. 1844.
26. Ibid., p. 1796.
27. Larson, *Contemporary Illustrations for Preachers, Teachers and Writers*, p. 47.
28. Jack Canfield, Mark Victor Hansen, Jennifer Read Hawthorne and Marci Shimoff, *Chicken Soup for the Mother's Soul* (Deerfield Beach, FL: Health Communications, Inc., 1997), p. 20.

CHAPTER THIRTEEN

I Go A-Fishing

*Much of the insight for this chapter was received while
listening to a tape by my brother, Tim Sheets. Thanks, Tim,
for the revelation of the Holy Spirit which flows through you.*

"I go a-fishing" (John 21:3, *KJV*). These were the words of Peter
during the most strategic span of days the human race has ever
known. Jesus had died, risen again and was about to ascend to
heaven and send the Holy Spirit back to birth His Church.

But Peter had had enough. It was all just a little too confusing.

- *Gethsemane:* Peter watched the Master repeatedly fall
  on His face, desperate, bloody, asking His Father to
  remove some cup from Him.
- *The Arrest:* Peter was ready to fight for his beloved
  Lord. He cut off the ear of one of the high priest's men.
  But Jesus put it back. He was *allowing* them to take
  Him. What was He doing? Why was this happening?
- *The Flight and Denial:* Yes, he had done it—just as the
  Master had predicted. With a curse, Peter had denied
  that he even knew Christ. The shame was too much. He
  went to a lonely place and "wept bitterly" (Luke 22:62).

- *The Beating:* Things had gone from bad to worse. The Lord—He whom they had believed to be the Messiah—was lashed with the hideous Roman cat-o-nine-tails. His body was a piece of raw meat, shreds of skin hanging from His lacerated flesh. His face was bruised, covered with spittle, and portions of His beard were torn from His face. Long thorns pierced deeply into His scalp. Blood flowed freely. What went wrong? They had watched Him heal lepers, open blind eyes, raise the dead to life, walk on water and calm storms. Just a few days ago He had demonstrated such strength as He cleansed the Temple for the second time, calling it "My house" (Luke 19:46). Now, all seemed lost. Surely the Master would do something soon. He would use His supernatural power and reverse this tragic turn of events.

- *The Cross:* But no, everything crashed. The Master was killed. Roman crucifixion, no less. The shame, suffering and cruelty was overwhelming. He died there—and, with Him, all of their hopes and dreams. It was over.
- *The Resurrection:* But maybe not. He had risen from the dead, or so it seemed. Someone claiming to be Him had walked through the wall into the place they were hiding and tried to minister peace. A week later He did it again. It seemed like Him, looked like Him, sounded like Him—He even showed them the wounds in His hands and side. But then He vanished again.

This was all too much for Peter. The highs too high, the lows too low. The plan was all messed up, the dreams shattered. And even if it had been Him, He was gone. They had lived with Him, walked with Him, listened to Him, watched Him minister. They had been together almost day and night for three years. They had left family, homes and businesses. And for what?

No, it was all too confusing, overwhelming and complicated for an uneducated fisherman from Galilee. What to do? Where to turn?

The twelve had separated now. The small group hanging out together looked to Peter for advice—he had risen as a leader among them. "What do you think, Peter? What should we do now?"

"I don't know about the rest of you," Peter answered. "But I'm going back to the only thing I know. Back to what I did before this confusing ride began. I'm goin' fishin'."

"Yeah, we'll go with you," they answered. And back to the boats they went.

I did this once. Throughout a period of several months, I prayed faithfully for a man who had terminal cancer. We became friends. I went time and time again to his home, shared the Word of God with him and prayed fervently for a miracle.

I spent the last three days of the man's life in his basement, praying all day long each day for a breakthrough. When he died, I was the first one called. I arrived before they removed his lifeless body from the home, gathered his wife, son and daughter to me and we prayed. In our pain and loss, we worshiped God and released this man into His care.

I was physically drained and emotionally spent. "What are you doing?" Ceci asked later that morning as I loaded some things in the car.

"I'm goin' fishin'," I said. And that's exactly what I did.

Why? I don't know why. I just needed to get away, to find solitude, to think, daydream, sort things out. I wasn't really fishing—I forgot all about the float bobbing up and down—I was searching. For answers. For an anchor—something familiar to grab hold of. For peace in the storm—some security during this time of pain and confusion. I wasn't trying to forget my friend; I was trying to deal with my pain.

Multiply this a hundred times and you may grasp something of the emotional trauma experienced by Peter. He was doing all he knew to do, reaching for the familiar, anything to bring a small sense of order and hope to his confused, chaotic world. "I go a-fishing."

To one degree or another we've all been there. A season of pain, loss, despair, confusion, dryness. Seasons of drought, darkness, winter. Remember, last year in America more than half of all pastors considered leaving the ministry—"I go a-fishing."

Drought-Resistant Spiritual Landscaping

We all can go through seasons of dryness in our walks with God. Winter seasons when there appears to be no life. Times when the river of Ezekiel 47 is in its trickle stage, if that. I've known times when a trickle would have been welcome.

Oh, I fight the good fight of faith, sometimes even relying on denial. At times I remind myself of the fighting fellow Mark Twain described: "Thrusting my nose firmly between his teeth, I threw him heavily to the ground on top of me."[1] I confess my victory and stand on the promises, but at times my circumstances continue to be dry.

These periods of dryness have many causes, ranging from sin to pain to character development. We may go through a time of dryness because we have compromised the basic disciplines of the faith—prayer, Bible reading, fellowship with others—or due to pain and loss. God also allows winter seasons to do some internal work in us, pruning and disciplining for future fruit.

David went through a dry season in Psalm 23, probably due to stress and fatigue. He said in verse 3, "He restores my soul." Interestingly, this restoration happened at the river—"beside the quiet waters." In Psalm 51, David's condition was caused by sin. In his prayer of repentance he cried out, "Restore to me the joy of Thy salvation" (v. 12).

The church at Ephesus was in a dry time, having left their *first* love (see Rev. 2:4). Here, the Greek word *protos* means first in a comparative sense, as in priority. Their priorities were messed up. God had been displaced. Perhaps too much religious activity had replaced relationship (see Rev. 2:2,3), or maybe there was disillusionment caused by the false apostles mentioned in verse 2. Many in the Church today are in dry times due to disillusionment and misplaced affections.

Others go through difficult times due to accidents and other adverse circumstances of life. Such was the case with Glenn Cunningham.

After suffering severe burns on his legs at the age of five, Glenn Cunningham was given up on by doctors who believed he would be a hopeless cripple destined to spend the rest of his life in a wheelchair. "He will never be able to walk again," they said. "No chance."

The doctors examined his legs, but they had no way of looking into Glenn Cunningham's heart. He didn't listen to the doctors and set out to walk again. Lying in bed, his skinny, red legs covered with scar tissue, Glenn vowed, "Next week, I'm going to get out of bed. I'm going to walk." And he did just that.

His mother tells of how she used to push back the curtain and look out the window to watch Glenn reach up and take hold of an old plow in the yard. With a hand on each handle, he began to make his gnarled and twisted legs function. And with every step a step of pain, he came closer to walking. Soon he began to trot; before long he was running. When he started to run, he became even more determined.

"I always believed that I could walk, and I did. Now I'm going to run faster than anybody has ever run." And did he ever.

He became a great miler who, in 1934, set the world's record of 4:06. He was honored as the outstanding athlete of the century at Madison Square Garden.[2]

Someone once said that pain is inevitable, suffering is optional. Personally, I have gone through dry periods when for weeks or months there was little emotion in my walk with God. No excitement, no exhilaration in my worship times, the Word seeming lifeless—all because God was developing character in me through a season of walking totally by faith. And during these dull, emotionless seasons I have experienced some of my greatest spiritual growth. I frequently return from these wilderness experiences as Jesus did, "in the power of the Spirit" (Luke 4:14) and moving in a greater anointing (see Luke 4:18,19).

Perhaps this is what Allyson Jones was thinking about when she said, "If I could wish for my life to be perfect, it would be tempting but I would have to decline, for life would no longer teach me anything."[3] The following story illustrates the potential for obstacles to become blessings:

> In ancient times, a king had a boulder placed on a roadway. Then he hid himself and watched to see if anyone would remove the huge rock. Some of the kingdom's wealthiest merchants and courtiers came by and simply walked around it. Many loudly blamed the king for not keeping the roads clear, but none did anything about getting the big stone out of the way. Then a peasant came along, carrying a load of vegetables. On approaching the boulder, the peasant laid down his burden and tried to move the stone to the side of the road. After much pushing and straining, he finally succeeded.
>
> As the peasant picked up his load of vegetables, he noticed a purse lying in the road where the boulder had been. The purse contained many gold coins and a note from the king indicating that the gold was for the person who removed the boulder from the roadway.
>
> The peasant learned what many others never understand: Every obstacle presents an opportunity to improve one's condition.[4]

A Season of Rest—
or the Sleep of Complacency?

Simply stated, there are seasons in our walks with God. Different seasons. Necessary seasons. Some are fun, exciting, wonderful; others are dry and difficult. There are four seasons climatically, and all are important. Spring is needed for sowing, summer for growing, fall for reaping and winter for rest. We are much the same. There are times to sow, times to reap, times for plowing, and times for resting. Times to enjoy, times to endure, times of great victory and times of learning to overcome.

Many in the Body of Christ are living through winter seasons. Some are cold, maybe even frozen. Others are very dry. Many are in a state of hibernation, sleeping their way through the season.

Another condition associated with winter is dormancy. This can be a sleep of complacency, or it could be a God-ordained season of inactivity for the purpose of rest. The word "dormitory"—a place of sleep or rest—is derived from the word "dormant." But those who have allowed the sleep of complacency to overtake them are like tame geese.

> Ronald Meredith, in his book *Hurryin' Big for Little Reasons*, describes one quiet night in early spring:
> Suddenly out of the night came the sound of wild geese flying. I ran to the house and breathlessly announced the excitement I felt. What is to compare with wild geese across the moon?
> It might have ended there except for the sight of our tame mallards on the pond. They heard the wild call they had once known. The honking out of the night sent little arrows of prompting deep into their wild yesterdays. Their wings fluttered a feeble response. The urge to fly—to take their place in the sky for which God made them—was sounding in their feathered breasts, but they never raised from the water.
> The matter had been settled long ago. The corn of the barnyard was too satisfying. Now their desire to fly only made them uncomfortable.[5]

Don't let anything—especially complacency—rob you of your desire to fly.

Unlike complacency, some dormancy is of God. Seeds go through dormancy and can actually remain in this condition for thousands of years. Some seeds found in Egyptian tombs have been planted and found to grow normally.

I have promise "seeds" entombed in me—words God has spoken to my heart—for which I have waited many years. I have vision seeds still dormant in me, waiting for God's time. I have planted seeds in others which lie dormant, the Spirit of God awaiting His opportunity to awaken them.

This truth is powerfully illustrated by Chrystle White in the following story:

In 1965 during a family reunion in Florida, my grandmother woke everyone at 2:00 A.M. issuing orders to get empty Coke bottles, corks and paper. "I've received a message from God," she said. "People must hear his word." She wrote verses on the paper, while the grandchildren bottled and corked them. Then everyone deposited over 200 bottles into the surf at Cocoa Beach.

People contacted and thanked my grandmother for the Scriptures throughout the years. She died in November 1974. The next month the last letter arrived:

Dear Mrs. Gause,

I'm writing this letter by candlelight. We no longer have electricity on the farm. My husband was killed in the fall when the tractor overturned. He left 11 young children and myself behind. The bank is foreclosing, there's one loaf of bread left, there's snow on the ground, Christmas is two weeks away. I prayed for forgiveness before I went to drown myself. The river has been frozen over for weeks, so I didn't think it would take long. When I broke the ice, a Coke bottle floated up. I opened it, and with tears and trembling hands, I read about hope. Ecclesiastes 9:4, "But for him who is joined to all the living there is hope..." Hebrews 7:19; 6:18; and John 3:3 were also referenced. I came home, read my Bible, and am thanking God. Please pray for us, but we're going to make it now. May God bless you and yours.   —A farm in Ohio[6]

How did that bottle get from Cocoa Beach, Florida, to a river in Ohio? God's angelic bottle patrol. I wonder how many bottles of word seeds those who teach and preach God's word have set afloat in people's minds—waiting for God's perfect timing. We never know when the seeds we plant will come to life, bringing spring to someone else's winter.

"Arise and Come Along!"

All of these thoughts about winter are very relevant to the river. The word used for "river" in Ezekiel 47 is *nachal* which means "a stream, especially a winter torrent."[7] Some streams and rivers are dry during certain times of the year. They fill up when there is rain or, as in this case, when the spring thaw melts the snow and ice on the mountains. Tiny rivulets form which come together to form streams and eventually rivers.

It is interesting that this is the type of river spoken of in Ezekiel 47. And fittingly, it begins as a trickle in verse 1, but eventually becomes a mighty, unfordable river by verse 5:

- For those who are confused and disillusioned...
- For the heart grieving from the pain of loss...
- For those asleep in the dormitory of complacency...
- For those who have misplaced their first love...
- For the faithful but weary soldier whose stream bed is dry...
- For those gone a-fishing...

It is time for the spring thaw!

Winter doesn't last forever. God is ready to bring the fire of His presence to melt the ice and snow of winter. The river will flow to us and through us. Dryness will end. Dormancy will yield to His command, "Arise, shine!" (Isa. 60:1). Seeds will come to life. Oppression will lift, joy will return. The internal dealings of the Spirit will become outward fruit.

No one imagined Charles Dutton would ever amount to any-

215

thing, for he spent many years imprisoned for manslaughter. When asked how he managed to make such a remarkable transition, this now-successful Broadway star replied, "Unlike the other prisoners, I never decorated my cell."[8]

I hope you haven't decorated your cell. The Song of Solomon 2:10-13 is taking place:

My beloved responded and said to me, "Arise, my darling, my beautiful one, and come along. For behold, the winter is past, the rain is over and gone. The flowers have already appeared in the land; the time has arrived for pruning the vines, and the voice of the turtledove has been heard in our land. The fig tree has ripened its figs, and the vines in blossom have given forth their fragrance. Arise, my darling, my beautiful one, and come along!"

For those who are in dry seasons as a result of sin, compromise or complacency, I like Psalm 51:1,10,12 from *The Message* by Peterson:

Generous in love—God, give grace! Huge in mercy—wipe out my bad record. God, make a fresh start in me, shape a Genesis week from the chaos of my life. Bring me back from gray exile, put a fresh wind in my sails!

God is ready to do just that.

If You Build It, He Will Come

What will bring the fire of Pentecost that brings the thaw? In the Old Testament, the fire of God fell on an altar and an acceptable sacrifice. In Genesis 15:17, the fire of God came on Abraham's sacrifice. In Leviticus 9:24, His fire fell and consumed the offering of Moses and Aaron. In Judges 6:21, fire sprang from the rock and consumed Gideon's sacrifice. Elijah, David and Solomon all had God answer by fire when acceptable sacrifices were offered.

What does an altar represent? A place of worship, consecration and rededication. A place to meet with God. And, yes, a place of death, where our lives are offered to Him. We are now the sacrifices that must be offered to God.

To offer their sacrifices, some of these men had to build altars, others had to repair altars and still others needed to tear down those erected for idolatry before replacing them with an altar to the Lord.

There was a movie a few years back entitled *Field of Dreams*, in which the main character had a dream of building a baseball diamond in a remote Iowa cornfield. An important line from the movie was, "If you build it, he will come." If you build an altar to the Lord—a place to meet with Him, a place of consecration, a place to lay your life down before Him—He will come. The God who answers by fire will consume the sacrifice, the thaw will begin, and the river will flow.

Elijah had to repair an altar before sacrificing to the Lord (see 1 Kings 18:30). Many in the Body of Christ have had altars in the past—places of intimacy with the Lord, strong prayer and devotional lives, strong commitments to the things of God—but they are currently in disrepair. Through neglect these altars have broken down and need rebuilding.

Repair them! Whatever the cost, rebuild the altar to God in your life!

As Elijah did, stand against the Ahabs, Jezebels and prophets of Baal and Asherah, and rebuild the altar. God will respond, the fire will fall, the thaw will occur, and the river will flow.

Gideon had to tear down an altar. He offered one sacrifice to the Lord, and it had been accepted. Before he could be used by God, however, he was told to:

"Take your father's bull and a second bull seven years old, and pull down the altar of Baal which belongs to your father, and cut down the Asherah that is beside it; and build an altar to the Lord your God on the top of this stronghold in an orderly manner, and take a second bull and offer a burnt offering with the wood of the Asherah which you shall cut down." Then Gideon took ten men of his servants and did as the Lord had spoken to him (Judg. 6:25-27).

Israel was so deep into sin they were worshiping Baal. (Talk about dry riverbeds!) And Gideon's family had so fallen into idolatry that the village shrine to Baal was in their backyard! No wonder God had given them into the hands of the Midianites. God, in essence, said to Gideon, "Baal must go before the Midianites go."

Anything we bow before, allowing it control in our lives, could be classified as an idol. Many have bowed to fear, unbelief, insecurity, past wounds, rejection, bitterness, selfish ambition, pride and a host of other things.

Tear these altars down! Then erect an altar to the living God. If you do, the fire will fall, the thaw will come, and the river will flow.

Become a Baal-conqueror. Gideon's name was changed to Jerubbaal, meaning Baal-conqueror, after he tore down the altar of Baal (see Judg. 7:1). Not only can God turn your winter into glorious spring, but if necessary He can transform you from a Baal-worshipper to a Baal-conqueror.

Your nature is to conquer (see Rom. 8:37). You are called to fly, not sit on the farm pond complacently reflecting back to your glory days of flight. Rise up!

Burn your fishing boat and throw away the nets! Your winter season is coming to an end. Our God in you is "a consuming fire" (Heb. 12:29). There is in you a river waiting to flow (see John 7:38).

If you build an altar, He will come.

If you repair and build, He will answer by fire.

If you tear down idolatrous altars, He will back you as He did Gideon, giving you a new name and a restored destiny.

Let the river flow!

Notes

1. T.P. Carter, *Jokes, Notes & Quotes* (Columbus, Georgia: Quill Publications, 1991), p. 213.
2. Jack Canfield, Mark Victor Hansen and Barry Spilchuk, *A Cup of Chicken Soup for the Soul* (Deerfield Beach, FL: Health Communications, Inc., 1996), pp. 70, 71.
3. Ibid., p. 75.
4. Ibid., p. 84.
5. Craig Brian Larson, *Illustrations for Preaching and Teaching* (Grand Rapids: Baker Books, 1993), p. 38. Adapted.
6. Canfield, *A Cup of Chicken Soup for the Soul*, pp. 186, 187. Adapted.
7. James Strong, *The New Strong's Exhaustive Concordance of the Bible* (Nashville: Thomas Nelson Publishers, 1990), ref. no. 5158.
8. Larson, *Illustrations for Preaching and Teaching*, p. 280. Adapted.

Bibliography

Barna, George. *How to Increase Giving in Your Church*. Ventura: Regal Books, 1997.

Barnhouse, Donald Grey. *Let Me Illustrate*. Grand Rapids: Fleming H. Revell, 1967.

Barnicle, Mike. "Commentary." *The Gazette* (Colorado Springs), February 16, 1998.

Barrett, David. *Our Globe and How to Reach It*. Birmingham: New Hope Publishing, 1991.

Bounds, E.M. *Power Through Prayer*. Grand Rapids: Baker Book House, 1977.

Bromiley, Geoffrey W. *Theological Dictionary of the New Testament, Abridged*. Grand Rapids: William B. Eerdmans Publishing Co., 1985.

Brown, Michael L. *From Holy Laughter to Holy Fire*. Shippensburg, PA: Destiny Image Publishers, Inc., 1996.

Bullinger, Ethelbert. *A Critical Lexicon and Concordance to the English and Greek New Testament*. Grand Rapids: Zondervan Publishing House, 1975.

Canfield, Jack and Hansen, Mark Victor. *Chicken Soup for the Soul*. Deerfield Beach, FL: Health Communications, Inc., 1993.

———. *A Third Serving of Chicken Soup for the Soul*. Deerfield Beach, FL: Health Communications, Inc., 1996.

Canfield, Jack; Hansen, Mark Victor; and Spilchuk, Barry. *A Cup of Chicken Soup for the Soul*. Deerfield Beach, FL: Health Communications, Inc., 1996.

Canfield, Jack; Hansen, Mark Victor; Hawthorne, Jennifer Read; and Shimoff, Marci. *Chicken Soup for the Mother's Soul*. Deerfield Beach, FL: Health Communications, Inc., 1997.

Carter, T.P. *Jokes, Notes and Quotes*. Columbus, Georgia: Quill Publications, 1991.

Chevreau, Guy. *Catch the Fire*. Toronto: HarperCollins Publishers, Ltd., 1994.

Conner, Kevin. *The Feasts of Israel*. Portland: Bible Temple Publications, 1980.

———. *The Tabernacle of Moses*. Portland: Bible Temple Publications, 1974.

The Consolidated-Webster Encyclopedic Dictionary. Chicago: Consolidated Book Publishers, 1954.

Damazio, Frank. *Seasons of Revival*. Portland: Bible Temple Publishing, 1996.

Dobson, Shirley. "America, Return to God." *Pray*, March/April 1998.

Finney, Charles G. *Revival Lectures*. Old Tappan, NJ: Fleming H. Revell Company.

Foster, Elon. *6000 Classic Sermon Illustrations*. Grand Rapids: Baker Books, reprinted 1993.

Harris, R. Laird; Archer Jr., Gleason L.; and Waltke, Bruce K. *Theological Wordbook of the Old Testament*. Chicago: Moody Press, 1980.

Larson, Craig Brian. *Contemporary Illustrations for Preachers, Teachers and Writers*. Grand Rapids: Baker Books, 1996.

———. *Illustrations for Preaching and Teaching*. Grand Rapids: Baker Books, 1993.

Lucado, Max. *And the Angels Were Silent*. Portland: Multnomah Press, 1992.

Mahoney, Ralph. *Is a New Wave of Revival Coming?* Burbank: World Missionary Assistance Plan, 1982.

McDowell, Josh and Hostetler, Bob. *Right from Wrong*. Dallas: Word Publishing, 1994.

New Geneva Study Bible. Foundation for Reformation, Thomas Nelson Publishers, 1995.

New Webster's Dictionary and Thesaurus of the English Language. New York: Lexicon Publications, Inc., 1991 edition.

Otis Jr., George. *The Last of the Giants*. Tarrytown, NY: Fleming H. Revell Company, 1991.

Pickett, Fuchsia. *The Next Move of God*. Lake Mary, FL: Creation House, 1994.

Riss, Richard M. "Evangelical Heroes Speak." *Destiny Image Digest*, fall 1997.

Rowell, Edward K. *Fresh Illustrations for Preaching and Teaching*. Grand Rapids: Baker Books, 1997.

———. *Quotes & Idea Starters for Preaching and Teaching*. Grand Rapids: Baker Books, 1996.

Strong, James. *The New Strong's Exhaustive Concordance of the Bible*. Nashville: Thomas Nelson Publishers, 1990.

Swindoll, Charles R. *Intimacy with the Almighty*. Dallas: Word Publishing, Inc., 1996.

Towns, Elmer L. and Anderson, Neil T. *Rivers of Revival*. Ventura: Regal Books, 1997.

Twenty-Six Translations of the Bible. Atlanta: Mathis Publishers, 1985.

Zodhiates, Spiros. *Hebrew-Greek Key Study Bible—New American Standard*. Chattanooga: AMG Publishers, 1984; revised edition, 1990.

———. *The Complete Word Study Dictionary*. Iowa Falls, Iowa: Word Bible Publishers, Inc., 1992.

Word Index

224

Scripture Index

Old Testament

New Testament